A Yeoman's Letters

P. T. Ross

In the interest of creating a more extensive selection of rare historical book reprints, we have chosen to reproduce this title even though it may possibly have occasional imperfections such as missing and blurred pages, missing text, poor pictures, markings, dark backgrounds and other reproduction issues beyond our control. Because this work is culturally important, we have made it available as a part of our commitment to protecting, preserving and promoting the world's literature. Thank you for your understanding.

A YEOMAN'S LETTERS

BY

P. T. ROSS

(Late Corporal 69th Sussex Company I.Y.)

ILLUSTRATED by the AUTHOR.

> "And you, good Yeomen,
> Whose limbs were made in England, show us here
> The mettle of your pasture; let us swear
> That you are worth your breeding; which I doubt not.
> *Shakespeare.*

THIRD EDITION.

LONDON:

SIMPKIN, MARSHALL, HAMILTON,
KENT & Co., LIMITED.

1901.

Warschawski.   St. Leonards-on-Sea.

CORPL. P. T. ROSS.

ILLUSTRATIONS.

	PAGE
"A Hot Time!"	2
"A Camp Sing-Song"	7
"The Great Small Game Quest(ion)"	9
"The Mealie and Oat Fatigue"	23
"Stable Guard"	31
"A Terrible Reckoning"	44
"Some of the Pomp and Circumstance of Glorious War"	52
"A New Rig-out"	58
"Oliver Twist on the Veldt"	65
"Hate"	68
"Mails Up"	87
"I'kona"	89
"Nobby"	94
"Consolation"	112
"On Pass"	114
"A Peep at Our Domestic Life"	118
"Hymns and their Singers"	129
"A Friendly Boer Family"	141
"Well, it's the best Oi can do for yez"	144
"Sick" and "Who said C.I.V.'s?"	148
"Got His Ticket"	153
"The Thoughtless Sister"	156
"God Save the King"	159
"Tommy's Spittoon"	171

FOREWORD.

"More khaki," sniffed a bored but charming lady, as she glanced at a picture of the poor Yeomanry at Lindley, and then hastily turned away to something of greater interest. I overheard the foregoing at the Royal Academy, soon after my return from South Africa, last May, and thanked the Fates that I was in mufti. It was to a certain extent indicative of the jaded interest with which the War is now being followed by a large proportion of the public at home, the majority of whom, I presume, have no near or dear ones concerned in the affair; a public which cheered itself hoarse and generally made "a hass" of itself many months ago in welcoming certain warriors whose period of active service had been somewhat short. I wonder how the veterans of the Natal campaign, the gallant Irish Brigade, and others, will be received when they return? "Come back from the War! What War?"

And yet in spite of this apathy, "War Books" keep appearing, and here is a simple Yeoman thrusting yet another on the British Public. Still 'twere worse than folly to apologise, for *qui s' excuse, s' accuse.*

The present unpretentious volume is composed of letters written to a friend from South Africa, during the past twelve months, with a few necessary omissions and additions; the illustrations which have been introduced, are reproductions in pen and ink of pencil sketches done on the veldt or in hospital. The sole aim throughout has been to represent a true picture of the every-day life of a trooper in the Imperial Yeomanry. In many cases the "grousing" of the ranker may strike the reader as objectionable, and had this record been penned in a comfortable study, arm-chair philosophy might have caused many a passage to be omitted. But the true campaigning atmosphere would have been sacrificed.

As the Sussex Squadron of Imperial Yeomanry was, in popular parlance, "on its own" till the end of May, the letters dealing with that period have been excluded. However, a brief account of the doings of the Squadron up to that time is necessary to give continuity to the story, so here it is:

The Sussex Yeomanry.

The Yeomanry is a Volunteer Force, and as is generally known, was embodied in Great Britain during the wars of the French Revolution. History records that at the period named, the County of Sussex possessed one of the finest Corps in England. *Autres temps, autres moeurs*, and so from apathy and disuse the Sussex Yeomanry gradually dwindled in numbers and importance, until it eventually became extinct. Then came the dark days of November and December, in the year eighteen-hundred-and-ninety-nine. Who will ever forget them? And who does not remember with pride the great outburst of patriotism, which, like a volcanic eruption, swept every obstacle before it, banishing Party rancour and class prejudice, thus welding the British race in one gigantic whole, ready to do and die for the honour of the Old Flag, and in defence of the Empire which has been built up by the blood and brains of its noblest sons. The call for Volunteers for Active Service was answered in a manner which left no doubt as to the issue. From North, South, East, and West, came offers of units, then tens, then hundreds, and finally, thousands, the flower of the Nation, were in arms ready for action. The Hon. T. A. Brassey, a Sussex man, holding a commission in the West Kent Yeomanry, applied for permission and undertook, early in February, 1900, to form a squadron of Yeomanry from Sussex. The enlistment was principally done at Eastbourne, as were also the preliminary drills. We went into quarters at Shorncliffe where we trained until the last week in March, when early, very early, one dark cold morning, a wailing sleepy drum and fife band played us down to the Shorncliffe Station, where we entrained for the Albert Docks, London. There the transport "Delphic" received us, together with a squadron of Paget's

Horse (the 73rd I.Y.), and soon after noon the officers and troopers were being borne down the river, and with mixed feelings, were beginning to realise they were actually off at last. Many, alas, were destined never to return.

It is more amusing than ever, now, to recall the remarks of cheerful, chaffing friends, who indulged in sly digs at the poor Yeomen previous to their departure. At that time, as now, "the end was in sight" only we had not got used to it. It was a common experience to be greeted with, "Ha, going out to South Africa! Why it'll be all over before you get there," or "Well, it'll be a pleasant little trip there and back, for I don't suppose they'll land you." Subsequent experience of troopships has dispelled even "the pleasant trip" illusion. Another favourite phrase, was "Well, if they do use you, they'll put you on the lines of communications." Sometimes a generous friend would confidentially ask, "Do you think they'll let you start?" And one, a lady, anxious on account of gew-gaws, observed, "Oh, I hope they'll give you a medal."

Eventually the slow but sure S.S. "Delphic," having stopped at St. Helena to land bullocks for Cronje, Schiel and their friends, disgorged us at Cape Town. Our anxiety as to whether the war was over was soon allayed, and we gaily marched, a perspiring company, to Maitland Camp. Here amid sand and flies we began to conceive what the real thing would be like. An extract or two from letters written while at that salubrious spot may serve to give an idea of the life there:

"This place is a perfect New Jerusalem as regards Sheenies, every civilian about the camp appearing to be a German Jew refugee. They have stalls and sell soap, buns, braces, belts, &c., and so forth. Every now and again a big Semitic proboscis appears at our tent door, and the question 'Does anypody vant to puy a vatch' is propounded."

Hungarian horses were drawn and quartered by our lines, and saddlery served out. By-the-way, I have always flattered myself there was at least one good thing about the 69th Squadron I.Y., they had excellent saddles. The first time we turned out in full marching order was a terrible affair, and the following may help to convey an idea of the *tout ensemble* of an erstwhile peaceful citizen:

"Please imagine me as an average Yeoman in full marching order. Dangling on each side of the saddle are apparently two small hay-ricks in nets; then wallets full, and over them a rolled overcoat and an extra pair of boots. Behind, rolled waterproof-sheet and army blanket, with iron picketing-peg and rope, and mess-tin on top. Elsewhere the close observer mentally notes a half-filled nosebag. So much for the horse, and then, loaded with the implements of war, bristling with cartridges, water-bottle, field-glass, haversack, bayonet and so on, we behold the Yeoman. With great dexterity (not always) he fits himself into the already apparently superfluously-decorated saddle, and once there, though he may wobble about, takes some displacing.

I really must remark on the marvellous head for figures that we Yeomen are expected to have. Read this. Comment from myself will be superfluous.

"My Company number is 51.
"My regimental number is 16,484.
"My rifle and bayonet, 2,502.
"The breech-block and barrel of the rifle are numbered 4,870.
"My horse's number is 1,388.
"There may be a few more numbers attached to me; if so, I have overlooked them."

En passant, I must mention we were with our proper battalion, the 14th, commanded by Colonel Brookfield, M.P., at Maitland. Eventually, thanks to the fact of his Grace the Duke of Norfolk being attached to our squadron, when we got the order to go up country we left the rest of the battalion behind at Bloemfontein, cursing, and proceeded by rail as far as Smaldeel, where we detrained with our horses and commenced treking after the immortal " Bobs."

His Grace's servant, rather an old fellow, did not seem to particularly care for campaigning, and, often, dolefully regarding his khaki garments, would sorrowfully remark, "To think as 'ow I've served 'im all these years, and now 'e should bring me hout 'ere. It does seem 'ard." I think a pilgrimage would have been more to his liking.

Our first experience of "watering horses" on the trek was both interesting and exciting, it occurred at Smaldeel.

"The horses we proceeded to water at once; I had the pleasure of taking two and of proving the proverb, *re* leading horses to the water. *En route* were dead horses to the right and dead horses to the left; in the water, which was black, one was dying in an apparently contented manner, while another lay within a few yards of it doing the same thing in a don't-care-a-bit sort of way. Regarded from five hours later, I fancy my performances with the two noble steeds in my charge must have been distinctly amusing to view, had anyone been unoccupied enough to watch me. Vainly did I try to induce them to drink of the printer's-ink-like fluid, water and mud, already stirred up by hundreds of other horses. When they did go in, they went for a splash, a paddle, and a roll, not to imbibe, and I had to go with them a little way, nearly up to my knees, in the mud. I have arrived at the conclusion that the noble quadruped is not an altogether pleasant beast. Still, I suppose he has an opinion of us poor mortals. In death he is also far from pleasant, as was conclusively proved when night came on, and a dead one near us began to assert his presence with unnecessary emphasis. Phew! It's all very well saying that a live donkey is better than a dead lion, but judging from my experience of dead horses, which is just commencing, I should say that the dead lion would prove mightily offensive."

The water in the Free State, as a rule, was most unsatisfactory. Marching in the wake of an army of about 50,000 men, however, one would scarcely expect water to remain unstirred or unpolluted. I always found my tea or coffee more enjoyable when the water for it was drawn by somebody else. Even though that comrade would jestingly call it "Bovril," and unnecessarily explain that the pool it came from contained two dead horses and an ox.

One more extract and I have done.

"Yesterday (Friday, May 25th) we got as far as Leeum Spruit. So far they had succeeded in getting the railway in working order, but there the scene was one of utter destruction, three or four bridges being blown up, and the rails all twisted and sticking up in the air. Hundreds of Kaffirs were at work getting things straight, which to any ordinary person would seem impossible.

"It is a marvellous sight to see the convoys toiling in the track of Roberts' army, the blown-up bridges and rails, and the deserted farms. Of course, some are still inhabited. It may interest linguists and admirers of Laurence Sterne to know that the language of the British Army in South Africa is the same as it was with our army in Flanders in Uncle Toby's days—of course, allowing for an up-to-date vocabulary."

"Sunday, May 27th.—Up with the unfortunate early worm, as usual. Our *reveillé* generally consists of a shout and a kick, as our bugle is not used. It seems hard to realise that to-day is Sunday, and while the church bells at home are ringing, or the service is in progress, we dirty, unshaven beings, who once had part in the faraway life, are either riding or leading our horses across the flat and, in many places, charred veldt, past blown-up bridges, torn-up rails, convoys leisurely drawn by languid oxen, demolished houses, bleached bones of oxen, horses and mules, as well as the so-often-alluded-to dead beasts known by Tommy as " Roberts' Milestones," and all that goes to war—glorious war. We are making a fairly long march to-day, as we hope to catch Roberts at last. Anyhow, to-night should see us at the frontier—the Vaal River.

Part I.

ON THE TREK.

WITH ROBERTS.

The Occupation of Johannesburg.

ORANGE GROVE,
NEAR JOHANNESBURG.
Saturday, June 2nd, 1900.

On Monday, May 28th, at mid-day, we reached the Vaal River, where we stopped and took all our superfluous kit off the horses, which left us with one blanket per man; were provided with four biscuits each, rations for two days, and so with light hearts and saddles, we forded Viljoen's Drift; into the Transvaal—at last! We had a long march to catch Roberts, but this country provides one with heaps of things to break any monotony that might otherwise exist, for it is ever "'Ware wire," "'Ware hole," "'Ware rock," or "'Ware ant hill," and now and again in the thick, blinding cloud of reddish dust a man and horse go down, and another a-top of them. Soon after dark, nearly the whole of the veldt around us became illuminated, reminding me of a colossal Brock's Benefit or the Jubilee Fleet Illuminations. As a matter of fact, the veldt was a-fire. The effect was really wonderful. At about ten o'clock we reached the main body, and being informed that Roberts was about four miles ahead with the 11th Division, our captain decided to bivouac for the night, and catch him up in the morning. After ringing our horses, we wandered round in the dark, and finding a convenient cart in a barn, soon after had a good enough fire to cook some meat we managed to secure, and then, dead fagged, turn in to sleep. [Here I would fain mutter an aside. When I was at home, a certain jingo song was much sung, perhaps is still; it was entitled, "A hot time in the Transvaal to-night." I want to find the man who wrote that song, and get him to bivouac with us for a night, at this time of the year, with an overcoat and one blanket.]

"A hot time!"

We awoke well covered with frost, and the stars have seldom twinkled on a more miserable set of shivering devils than we of the 69th Company I.Y. A nibble at a biscuit, no coffee, and we were after Roberts. We caught him up after about an hour's riding; the 11th Division was moving out as we came up. The Guards' Brigade was going forward on our right, and Artillery rolling forward on our left, with ambulance waggons, carts, and general camp equipment joining in the procession. We moved smartly on, trotting past the Guards' Brigade, soldiers straggling on who had fallen out for one reason or another, or sitting by the wayside attending to sore feet, till we came up with the Staff. Our captain reported himself, and *pro tem.* we were attached to Lord Roberts' bodyguard.

After a halt for our mid-day grub (we had none, having devoured our biscuits and emergency rations about three hours before, for which we were severely reprimanded by our captain, the Hon. T. A. B.), we proceeded again. At last we reached a ridge, and halting there, we beheld the Rand, and about six miles to our left, Johannesburg. A railway station having been captured, with about a dozen engines and rolling stock, the Army bivouacked for the night. We were in a field by a farmhouse, where we bought some meat very cheaply, and had a good supper, which would have been all the better had we had bread or even the once but now no more despised biscuits to eat with it. The next day we received orders to join the 7th Battalion I.Y., so saddled up, and passing through Elsburg and the Rose Dip, Primrose, and other mines, joined our new Battalion at Germiston. The 7th I.Y. Battalion is a West Country one, being composed of the Devon, Dorset, and Somerset Yeomanry and has seen some stiff service at Dewetsdorp. In the afternoon I had the misfortune to go out with our troop officer and another man to find our 4th troop, which had been left behind as baggage guard. Us did he lose (oh, the Yeomanry officer!) and when it was dark, we set out to find our company in the great camp the other side of Elsburg. What I said about that officer as I stumbled over rocks, ant hills, and holes, in these, my cooler moments, it would not become my dignity to record. The next day, Thursday (my birthday) promised to be an eventful one, and was. Johannesburg was to be attacked if it did not surrender by ten o'clock. With well-cleaned rifles and tightly-girthed horses, we moved out with our Battalion at nine o'clock to take up our position. Our duty was to attack the waterworks, if there was any resistance. However, as you know, the place capitulated; news was brought to us that the fort had surrendered, and we at once rapidly trotted up to it to take possession. Arrived outside, we were dismounted and marched into it, and drawn up in line facing the flagstaff on the fort wall. Suddenly a little ball was run up to the truck, a jerk and the Flag of England, the dear old Union Jack, was flying on the walls of the Johannesburg Fort. Then we cheered for our Queen, and again, when from somewhere a chromo of Her Gracious Majesty was produced and held aloft. Roberts' Raid had been successful. The Boer garrison seemed more relieved than depressed. Indeed, the commandant's servant gave us all the cold roast beef and bread that he had. Guards having been told off, and the horses picketed in the Police Barracks Yard, some of us had leave to go into the town. I was one of the fortunates. The enthusiasm of the inhabitants and their generous treatment of the men in khaki will be long remembered. The coloured population all showed great, gleaming rows of teeth, and ejaculated what I took to be meant for British cheers. Bread was given away, cigars and cigarettes forced (?) upon us, and meals stood right and left. A German girl, at a florist's, decorated about half-a-dozen of us with red, white and blue buttonholes. We were dirty and unshaven, but it mattered not, we were monarchs *(Væ Victis!)* and was it not my birthday? Into the shops we went. All were closed, but we persuaded some to open, and the good German Jew merchants let us commandeer within reason. Haversacks and pockets were filled. The actual prices of things were fairly high: sugar 1/6 per lb., condensed milk 2/-, golden syrup 4/- a small tin, and so on. One of our fellows, after being well fed, was sent back to us loaded with boxes of briar pipes to distribute, another with socks and vests; others were given Kruger pennies, as souvenirs. And all the day, and all the night, through the streets marched our troops, rolled and rattled our guns, our carts and waggons. And the night, oh, what a night! For seven miles I struggled on in charge of our ammunition cart, in search of our company, picking my way out of a mass of bullock waggons, carts, mules, and every imaginable vehicle; men asking for this brigade and that division on every hand; transport officers cursing, conductors exhorting, and niggers yelling and cracking whips.

Pretoria Taken.

Within sight of Eerstie Fabriken,
E. of Pretoria.

June 10*th*, 1900.

Fortunately for you in my last I left off rather abruptly in order to catch the post, or I should have bored you with a long account of my search with our ammunition cart for the company along the road to Pretoria from Johannesburg. For seven miles we—a comrade, myself, the blank Kaffir driver and mules—struggled and stumbled between long halts after our crowd, past waggons, carts, dhoolies, and chaises of all descriptions, the drivers of most of which were all inquiring for various divisions, brigades, battalions, companies, and such like. At last, at about one o'clock, having come up with the 11th Division, we halted and outspanned near the Guards' Brigade. At the first sign of daybreak I arose, and going forward about a quarter of a mile or less, came up with our company. The captain told me to get the mules inspanned and follow on. Owing to the infernal slowness of Tom, the driver, we got off late and had another terrible search, this time by daylight, to find the 7th Battalion I.Y., which at last we found camped at Orange Grove, about two miles from where we had bivouacked the preceding night. The next day (Sunday) we were looking to spending in a restful way, but this was not to be. We suddenly got the order to "saddle up," and forward to Pretoria we went. At about two in the afternoon we halted and picketed our horses not far from a farm. There rather a curious, though perhaps trivial, thing happened. Amongst the hundred-and-one little *contretemps* to which the Imperial Yeoman on active service is heir to, I had lost my nosebag on our night march from Johannesburg. This contained, besides the horse's feed, a tin of honey—of which I am as fond as any bear—and a pot of bloater paste, obtained (good word) at the Golden City from a "Sherman Shoe." Well, wandering in the direction of the farm, I came near a duck-pond and a clump of small trees, from which smoke was arising. My curiosity being aroused, I approached, and found that some Australians and Cape Boys were smoking out some bees. I arrived in the nick of time, and got a helmet-full of the most delicious honey in the comb I have tasted for many a day. On Monday, June 4th, we started for what we understood was to be our last march to Pretoria. We had the good fortune to be in the advance party. Soon after starting the Duke of Norfolk's horse fell in a hole and put his thigh out, so he lost the fun, for it was not long before, from the hills ahead of us, came rap, rap, and then the rat-tat-tat-tat of a machine gun. We dismounted, advanced extended, and opened fire. I aimed at the hills, so I know I hit something. The Boers retiring, we (that is the battalion) occupied one kopje and then another, the dust flicking up in front of us. Then boom! whish-sh-sh! a cloud of red dust shot up, and crack! and their artillery had come into action. One shell burst directly over our heads, then we were told to retire to our led horses, which necessitated crossing a road on which their fire was directed. Needless to say this was not an altogether uninteresting proceeding. And so the game went on, our guns coming into action in grand style. We got in for rather a warm rifle fire once; we galloped up, dismounted, and advanced to the top of a kopje which was covered with rather long grass. Buzz-buzz-buzz went the busy bullets seeking unwilling billets. They came very close there, snipping the grass tops close beside us. Here there were casualties in several of the other companies. One of our fellows was shot through the leg, and Mr. Ashby was knocked on the waist-belt by a spent bullet or piece of shell and rendered unconscious for some time. Later, in galloping across an exposed space to occupy another kopje, the captain's horse was shot under him, as well as several others. I think that is more than enough of the affair; I have no doubt you know better what really was done than we. No waggons coming up that night, we had no rations nor breakfast next day, so you see we do the thing in style, for we had started the day at four and only had a pannikin of coffee and a biscuit for breakfast. The next day we heard that the Pretoria Forts had surrendered and the Boer Forces withdrawn, and the whole army advanced at last on its final march to Pretoria, and this humble *Ego*, who months ago at home had thought and talked of this great event, and not for a moment anticipated participation in the same, formed a modest unit of the victorious horde. However, that day we (the 7th I.Y.) did not go into the capital, but camped outside of it. Not to be done, after we had picketed our horses, I made my way into a Kaffir suburb

A Camp Sing Song
"They call me the Jewel of Asia."

near us, and did well at a couple of stores, kept by German Jews, coming back with a sack of tinned edibles and some Kruger pennies. The next day a friend and I were lucky, and got leave into Pretoria. We returned to a grateful and enthusiastic troop, laden with quite a score-and-a-half of loaves, at six in the evening, and concluded a pleasant day with a high tea (very high) and a camp-fire sing-song. "Chorus, gentlemen!":

It's 'ard to sye good-bye to yer own native land,
It's 'ard to give the farewell kiss, and parting grip of the 'and,
It's 'ard to leave yer sweetheart, in foreign lands to roam;
But it's 'arder still to sye good-bye to the ole folks at 'ome.

That night we entertained several ex-British soldier prisoners from Waterval.

My horse (late of the R.H.A.), picked up at Kroonstad, is going very strong. He is very useful to me as a means of locomotion, but otherwise no good feeling exists between us, for he is the most senseless, clumsy brute that I have ever come across in the animal kingdom. He is always treading on me and doing other idiotic and annoying acts. A few days ago he got entangled in the picketing ropes, and on my going to his assistance promptly fell forward upon me (he is the biggest horse I have seen in any Yeomanry Company) and nearly broke my instep. I have lately re-christened him "Juggernaut," which I think is not an inappropriate name. I had not much time to spare when we went into Pretoria, but could not help stopping to watch a couple of regiments go through—the Derbies with their band and the Camerons with their pipers. It was a grand sight to see those dirty, ragged, khaki-clad fellows tramping past the Volksraad, over which the Flag was flying, and note the tired but grim smile of satisfaction with which they regarded it. Quite two out of every four infantrymen I saw limped along with feet sore from marching over all sorts of roads and "where there was never a road." Some were getting along with the aid of sticks—most, if not all, of the officers march with sticks.

On Thursday, June 7th, we were still in camp outside of Pretoria, with a hospital, containing interesting cases of leprosy, small-pox and fever behind us; and about 200 yards to our left front hundreds of dead horses and a few vultures. At mid-day the usual unexpected thing happened, and it was "saddle up," and off we rode through the captured capital, passing Kruger's house, with the two lions outside the entrance, presented to him by Barney Barnato, and a group of typical old Boers seated at a table on the stoep. We bivouacked about six or eight miles east of the town, and the next morning caught up the army and took our place in advance again. At mid-day we halted within sight of Eerstie Fabriken.* Some of us were having a *siesta* and others eating biscuits and bully beef, or smoking the pipe of peace (peace, when there is no peace!), when—Boom! whish-sh! over our heads, and about 100 yards behind us a group of horses was lost in a cloud of brown earth and dust. Then another and another came, and we got the order to take cover to our right, which was promptly obeyed. Our guns came into action, and later an armistice was arranged, for the convenience of Brother Boer, I presume, which to-day (Sunday) still continues.

The Great Small Game Quest(ion)

This morning (Sunday, the 10th) we had the first Church Parade we have had for a long time. The sermon was good, and from it I gathered that it was Trinity Sunday.

---

* Otherwise known as the "Hatherly Distillery," owned by a chameleon millionaire German-Jew, named Sammy Marks. Oh, that fine old Scotch whisky! The labels announcing this un-fact are, I understand, obtained from the Old Country and gummed on the bottles at Hatherly.

Yesterday it was a curious sight to see us employing our leisured ease in stripping ourselves, scratching our bodies, and carefully examining our shirts and underwear. A brutal lice(ntious) soldiery! Most of us have had quite large families of *these* dependent upon us; a more euphonious term for them is "Roberts' Scouts." Men to whom the existence of such insects was once merely a vaguely-accepted fact, and who would have brought libel actions against any persons insinuating that they possessed such things, after having been disillusioned of the idea that they were troubled with the "prickly itch," were calmly, naked and unashamed, searching diligently for their tormentors in their clothes as to the manner born. Being fortunate enough to find an officer's servant with a bottle of Jeyes', I finally washed both myself and clothes in a solution of it, so once again I am a free man, but the cry goes up "How long?" and echo repeats it. I have been told that the best way to get rid of these undesirable insects is to keep turning one's shirt inside out; by this means *their hearts are eventually broken.*

Diamond Hill and After.[*]

PIENAARSPOORT.

Friday, June 15th, (?) 1900.

Dolce far niente. I am not certain about the spelling, or quite positive about its interpretation, but it means something comfortable, I am sure. And that is just what I am at present. I have lost the scanty notes on which I try to base my periodical literary outbursts, and which assist me to retain some hazy notion of the date and day of the week, so both you at home and I out here ought to feel "for this relief much thanks!" And the reason for all this contentment and satisfaction is this. We were shifted from our last camping ground yesterday afternoon, and have arrived here. We are here for two or three days at the least. That is as far as we can gather, and we "just do" hear a lot. This means a bit of rest from the everlasting early *reveillé*, saddling

[*] That we played a small part in the extensive operations, culminating in what is known as the Battle of Diamond Hill, was only known to most of us four or five months later.

up, packing up kit, and so forth. So behold me on the veldt, leaning against my saddle in my shirt sleeves, taking things easy, after having dined well on a loaf of bread well covered with tinned butter obtained at a store some miles back owing to my having to fall out of the ranks on account of a broken girth (hem!) on our march hither. The bread a Scotch farmer, and tenant of Sammy Marks, gave me yesterday. Of course you must have noted how the principal topic with us is grub, and probably felt contempt for us, still I assure you it is the great Army question. When you meet a man out here, usually the first question is "What sort of grub are you having?" Then, after another remark or so, "Seen much fighting?" Or, again, on asking a man what sort of a general Buller is, for instance, the reply comes pat, "A grand man—he looks after your rations. Feeds you well!" Still, it must be admitted it looks rather amusing to see a big, bearded man expectantly awaiting his share of condensed milk or sugar to spread on a piece of biscuit. As regards fighting, we have been shelled over a bit lately. I think it was last Monday I had to go and see if there was anybody in a small house some distance opposite a range of kopjes occupied by the enemy. I had to kick in the door, and hitch my horse to a tree. Nobody was in the house; but the firing got very warm while I was making my visit. On Tuesday one of our patrols was ambushed, and only one man returned with the news. Later the officer in command of the troop came in with a corporal, and we heard that one fellow had been severely wounded and several horses lost. The rest eventually straggled in. All had tales of marvellous escapes to tell, some had laid low in a river up to their necks in water for many hours, others in the long grass. Yesterday we heard that the Boers confessed to three killed and three or four wounded, and as our man is progressing favourably I don't think their ambush was a great success, especially as they opened fire at a hundred yards or less, a fact which does not speak highly for their marksmanship.

Referring to grass, it is truly wonderful how inconspicuous our khaki is amidst rocks or grass. Riding along on Monday last I almost rode slap over some Guardsmen who were halted and lying or sitting in the grass. I only became aware of their presence when about ten yards from them. And they all want to get home again—

"'Ome, and friends so dear, Jennie,
 'Anging round the yard,
All the way from Fratton,
 Down to Portsmouth 'Ard."

Nearly every other sentence one hears out here begins with "When I get home ——." Had one of the Guardsmen been inclined to assist me with a rhyme to the tune of "Mandalay," he might have sinned thuswise:

I'm learnin' 'ere in Afriky wot the bloomin' poet tells,
If you've 'eard the song of "'Ome, sweet 'Ome," you won't
 'eed nothin' else.
    No, you won't 'eed nothin' else
    But the English hills and dells,
And the cosy house or cottage where the lovin' family dwells.
    On the road to London Town,
    Home of great and small renown,
Where the bright lights gleam and glitter on the rich and on the poor.
    Oh! the lights of London Town,
    And the strollin' up and down,
Where the fog rolls over everything and the mighty city's roar.
Ship me home towards that city, where the best live with the worst,
Where there are "Blue Ribbon" Armies, but a man *can* quench
 a thirst.

This, by the way, might allude to Lord Roberts' order, by which all the bars are closed wherever the troops go. When I went into Pretoria not a bar was open.

"'E's rather down on drink
 Is Father Bobs."

It is quite on the cards that we may be disbanded soon. The war is generally regarded as almost over, and candidates for the Military Police Force, which is being organised for the Transvaal and Orange Free State, are being sought for amongst the various Yeomanry Companies out here, the conditions being an optional three months' service, ten shillings a day pay and all found. About fifty of our company have volunteered, and may go into Pretoria any day now. These fifty have been supplied with the best horses we have amongst us, and we have not many now, my horse "Juggernaut," being one of the horses which had to be handed to the future *slops*, as the candidates are now being disrespectfully termed. This being the case, my future movements will be in the manner called "a foot slog" behind the ox-waggons.

Back to Pretoria.

NEAR THE RACECOURSE, PRETORIA.
(A Return Visit.)
Wednesday, June 20th, 1900.

"Here we are again" at Pretoria, that is, all that is left of us, for about fifty have joined the Military Police, others are wounded, sick, or missing, and the horses now in our lines number about two dozen moderately sound ones. All of this suggests, to minds capable of the wildest imaginings, a near return to England, home, and beauty. Some experts have actually fixed the date, which varies from within the week to within the next two months.

Last Saturday (June 16th) we left Pienaarspoort in the morning, and marched for about five miles in an easterly direction, many of us doing "a foot slog," having, as I have already mentioned, surrendered our mounts to the policemen; the mounted men had only just unsaddled for the mid-day halt, and collected wood to cook coffee and in some cases ducks obtained from inhospitable farmers flying the white flag, an emblem of which the Boer has made the best use for himself times innumerable, when the order was heliographed from a distant kopje for the 7th Battalion I.Y., attached to the 4th M.I., to march back to Pretoria. Then, in my opinion, a great event happened. We footsloggers determined to detach ourselves from our particular convoy and march into Pretoria, a distance of twenty miles or more, in addition to the four we had already tramped. I believe it was in my brain that this memorable (to us) march originated. We were certain that the mounted men would not reach the capital that night, as of course they had to keep in touch with the ox-waggons, and as we had to tramp, we determined to tramp to some purpose. Our goal was no cold bivouac on the hard earth outside Pretoria, with the usual weary waiting for the ox-waggons stuck in a spruit about four miles astern, but Pretoria itself, where bread and stores were to be obtained, a square meal at a table, and, oh! ye gentlemen of England, who live at home at ease, *a bed*. Imbued with this idea, with sloped rifle we gaily commenced our return march. Soon we came upon miles upon miles of convoys with straggling Colonials, Highlanders, Guardsmen, C.I.V.'s, indeed, representatives of all branches of the service, and all parts of the Empire, one and all toiling in the direction of Pretoria. We started at about mid-day, and reached our destination, tired and famished, at seven. After the first ten miles, behold a string of four men, tramping with never a halt, over rocks and grass, through spruits, past unutterably aromatic defunct representatives of the equine race, and through dust ankle deep, towards the city of their desire. Darkness came on swiftly, as it does out here, and past hundreds of camp fires they limped, footsore but as determined as ever, though in no good temper, for this is the order of some of their questions and answers towards the end of their march:

"How far off is Pretoria?"—"Three-and-a-half miles."
"How far off is Pretoria?"—"Seven miles."
"How far off is Pretoria?"—"Nine miles."
"How far off is Pretoria?"—"Three miles."
"Have you a Kruger penny?"—"No."
After tramping another two miles:
"How far off is Pretoria?"—"Three or four miles."

At last we beheld lights, not camp lights, but electric lights, and cheered by these, we quickened our pace. Alas! they seemed to play us a sorry game, and mocking, Will-o'-the-Wisp-like, retreated as we advanced. Then, too, we cursed those once blessed electric lights. Finally we reached the outskirts of the town, and seeing a closed store, with rifle butts and threatening tones persuaded the German dealer to open unto us. Here, speaking personally, I disposed of over half a tin of biscuits and two tins of jam. *Note by the Way:* These South African fresh fruit jams are, I am convinced, made of the numberless pumpkins and similar vegetables that one sees in nearly every field, and then indiscriminately labelled (I nearly wrote *libelled*) "peach," "apricot," "greengage," and—so help me, Roberts!—"marmalade." One of the manufacturers even has the audacity to boldly proclaim his preserves "stoneless plum and apricot";—as a matter of fact, pumpkins do not usually have stones.

Finally we entered the town, where every shop was closed, but, thanks to the guidance of a kindly German, after about half-a-dozen unsuccessful efforts we at length obtained food and shelter at a house called "The Albion." Oh, the pleasure of sleeping in a bed and under a roof after *æons* (to me) on the hard earth beneath the stars and dew! The next morning (Sunday) as we were breakfasting, we beheld unseen, the 7th Battalion ride past, and later, after purchasing a few stores, joined them where they were camped near the now historic Racecourse. I omitted to mention above that as we lay in our comfortable beds that eventful Saturday night, we heard the rain pouring in torrents upon the galvanised iron roof above our heads, and grimly smiled as we thought of the other less fortunate officers, non-commissioned officers and men of the I.Y., lying out in the open, vainly trying to get shelter and protection under narrow waterproof sheets. Alas, we only had the laugh of them that night—I am writing on Friday, June 22nd—for since then we have had rain every night, and a fair amount in the daytime as well, and when it rains out here there is no compromise about it. Without tents we have had a "dooce" of a time. Of course, we have to improvise shelters with our blankets. Our place is known as "The Moated Grange,"—a trench having been dug round it for reasons not wholly connected with *Jupiter Pluvius*. Others are, or would be, known to the postman, did he but come our way ("he cometh not") as "No. 1 Park Mansions," "The Manor House," "Balmoral," "Belle Vue," "Buckingham Palace," and "The Lodge." *Apropos* of something which concerns a lot of A.M.B.'s, the following may not be devoid of interest:

Scene: Any chemist's shop in Pretoria. Enter gentleman in khaki shrugging himself. With a scratch at his chest and side.

"Er—have you any—er—Keating's powder?"

Chemist: "No, zaar, de Englis' soldiers haf bought it all. It is finish." (Exit gentleman in khaki, scratching himself desperately.)

Our numbers are now considerably reduced, over half of the Battalion have joined the Military Police, others having taken over civil employment in the Post Office and Government buildings. Many who were not desirous of joining the Police have finally done so, thanks to the innumerable fatigues, pickets on the surrounding kopjes, and the crowning discomforts of the rainy nights (now over, I am happy to say, Sunday, June, 24th). At present our particular, or unparticular, company, numbers twenty-one men, with five troop horses and some officers' chargers, all that is left of the hundred and twenty mounted men that left Maitland Camp in May. Does this sound Utopian? Those men who are anxious to obtain civil employment are allowed (or persuaded) to join the Police, while the authorities are exerting themselves to obtain berths for them at salaries ranging from £300 to £500 or more per annum. While nominally with the Police these men do no duties, but draw ten shillings a day, besides having the advantage, when it rains, of possessing a roof over their heads, and the pleasurable knowledge that their pig-headed comrades who have joined as Yeomen and elect to remain so to the end, are in the diminished lines about two miles out of the town, doing fatigues and guards innumerable, and drawing therefor the munificent sum of 1s. 5d. per *diem*. Every day for the last week the captain and officers have been asking the men if they wish to join the Police or would like to have civil employment found them; and the company has been more like a registry office than anything else I can think of. To-day (Sunday) we—nine of us and a sergeant—went to church with other detachments of the 7th I.Y. It was no open-air church parade, where one has to stand all through the service, but a genuine church with pews that we went to. It is called St. Alban's Cathedral, and is evidently the chief English Church in Pretoria. It was the first time we had been in a church since leaving Shorncliffe; the service was very reminiscent of a home one and exceedingly restful. The illusion was complete when, at the conclusion of the service, *a collection was taken*. Now that the rain is all over, we have had tents served out to us. The battalion sergeant-major came round a few days ago with "Now, then, you fellows, down with those *rabbit hutches* ("The Grange") and put these tents up." They are Boer tents, small and oblong in shape. Ours is very rotten, and has a big hole burnt in the top as well as a large rent at one end. These we have, however, patched up to our satisfaction and comfort. As we are here for the deuce knows how long, the beloved army red tape and routine is coming into vogue again.

Entertaining a Guest.

HOREN'S NEK,
(About 10 miles W. of Pretoria).
Thursday, July 5th, 1900.

Here goes for another letter, so pull yourself together. I am here with twenty others of the 7th I.Y. on outlying picket, and although the affair began rather joylessly, we are getting on very well now. By way of parenthesis, it is more than passing strange that whenever I try to write a letter somebody always starts singing. At present, a man of the Dorsets is lifting his voice in anguish and promising to "Take Kathleen home again." He has just followed on with that mournful ballad, entitled "The Gipsy's Warning :"
"Do not 'eed 'im, gentle strynger."
I cannot help heeding him, but I dare not remonstrate, as he is the cook of our party, and in the Army, as elsewhere, *Monsieur le Chef,* be he ever so humble, is a power. So I will desist for the present, and resume this to-morrow on the top of a kopje.

(Resumed.)

Every night we do guard on two of the near kopjes, and every other day I have to go up with a guard, to another kopje, used as an observation post, and look with a telescope and the nude optic, Sister Anne like, for "staggerers of humanity." On Sunday, the 1st, we went to church again. The preparations the young British Yeoman makes for church going out here vary considerably, like most other things, from those he is accustomed to make at home. Having shaved himself with the aid of the only piece of looking-glass possessed by the company, and a razor, which in days gone by would have been a valuable acquisition to the Inquisitorial torture chambers, washed in a bucket and brushed his clothes with an old horse brush, technically known as "a dandy," he looks like a fairly respectable tramp, and is ready to fall in with his comrades for the two or three miles tramp to Divine service. I had the pleasure of entertaining a guest at breakfast before going to kirk. He rode up to our cook-house fire (one always *says* cook-house and guard-room) to get a light for his pipe. The broad-brimmed hat with the bronze badge of maple leaves and the word "*Canada*," proclaimed whence he hailed. After a few minutes' conversation, I invited him to partake of our breakfast, and, after no little persuasion—he at first refused on the grounds that he would be depriving us of our full share—he accepted, and came and joined us. He seemed very reluctant to take much at first, and all through the meal, which consisted of mealie porridge and sugar, *café sans lait*, bread and jam, expressed his appreciation of our scant hospitality. He had joined the Military Police for three months, and was on patrol.

"Where did he hail from?"

"The North-West Frontier."

"Had he ever been to England?"

"No; but would like to, I guess."

Here was a man who had never seen England, roughing it and fighting for her out here, side by side with us, the home-born; and he only one of many.

"Hang it, have some more jam, old chap?"

He told us all about the life (cow-boy) he led at home, and wished he could have our company at a "rounding-up," it was rare fun.

* * * * * * *

"Now, then, turn out, and get everything packed on the waggons at once, and fall in in marching order!" How would you like to be awakened out of a comfortable sleep at 3 a.m. in the above manner? Still, we are pretty well accustomed to that sort of thing by now. Having fulfilled the above injunctions, we stood to arms for about three hours and were then dismissed. Some of us, I being one, were told off for the outlying picket we are now doing. *Just* as dinner was served up, we had to fall in and march off, so, despite a ravenous appetite, I had to throw the contents of my pannikin, which I had just filled, away, and with smothered curses on the usual "messing about" which the Imperial Yeoman always has to suffer, fell in and marched away. When we reached this place at about five o'clock, we found that, owing to the usual somebody blundering, sufficient rations had not been put on the waggons for us. The men we relieved seemed very unhappy and were delighted to hear they were to go back. They had had one or two alarms, and had to retire on a fort one night. Almost immediately we were sent off to our kopjes, where we spend our nights. The kopjes round here are really horrible things: to ascend and descend them one requires legs of flexible iron, and the amiability and patience of Job. At night one has to pick and choose a little, before getting a satisfactory "doss." To arrange your couch you must, of course, remove all the movable stones, and as regards the fixtures it is strange how in a short time one's body seems instinctively to accommodate itself to the undulations of the chosen sleeping ground. It is strange also how a rock with a few handfuls of grass makes a fairly decent pillow.

Near here there are numerous orange groves lying in the shelter of the kopjes. Yesterday I had charge of a Dutchman who wanted to go through the Nek on business, and on the off chance I went provided with a nosebag. I came across a magnificent orange grove, owned, as it proved, by an Englishman who had been, he told me, out here for twenty-five years. This Englishman sent one of his sons off to fill my bag with the best oranges, and another to fill my red handkerchief with mealie meal to make porridge with. The red-handkerchief-with-white-spots alluded to above is the last "wipe" I have left me out of a large number, and has been invaluable to me on numerous occasions for carrying various articles, usually edible. On the whole, the time I have spent on this outpost has been rather enjoyable. Having only one officer with us, and being a reasonable distance from headquarters, we have been spared a great deal of the "messing about" which seems to be the special fate of the Imperial Yeomen. When you get your British Yeomen home again, many a tale of incompetent officers and needless hardships will be retailed, unless I am much in error. Here is apparently a small fact, which may help to show *why* the Yeoman has often fared worse than his regular brother. The quartermaster-sergeant of a certain I.Y. company I know of, is, like most others, a man absolutely unaccustomed to and unqualified for the job. Added to this, the disposition of the man is of such a nervous nature that he is afraid to try and work on his own initiative, and consequently when requisitioning for his company's rations, he not only fails to do what his regular brother non.-com. would do, viz. : get as much as he can for his company, but fails often to requisition or obtain their bare allowance. Once I met and asked this man if he had drawn any jam for his company's tea, and his sleepily-drawled reply was, "No-o, we were entitled to it, but I forgot to draw it." He forgot, and a hundred hungry men were dependent on the energy of such a man. Compare this amateur quartermaster-sergeant to the professional one, and you can plainly see one way in which Thomas Atkins scores over his Yeoman brother. Again, the two cooks of the same company were admittedly the slackest and dirtiest men of the lot (the only qualification necessary for a Yeomanry cook is the capability to boil water, and some seldom achieve records even in doing that). Thanks to their dirtiness, the thirsty troopers more often than not, had their tea or coffee spoilt owing to the greasy state of the dixies (cooking pots), which had not been cleaned after boiling the trek ox stew in them.

I am almost baking on the top of this kopje, as I sit with my back against a rock and indite these little records. It seems hard to imagine that early every morning muffled-up, shivering forms wait anxiously for King Sol to stick his dear, red, blushing face above yonder range of kopjes to warm us with his genial presence. Yesterday we had some of Plumer's men in our little camp. They were rattling good fellows, and had had a very hot time. They assured us that when they entered Mafeking, so tired and gaunt were they, owing to their living on short commons for so long, that any stranger might well have mistaken them for the relieved garrison, and the garrison for the relieving force. They also said the fellows there did not look half so bad as one would have imagined, though they had eaten nearly every horse and mule in the place. The idea which seemed general, that Plumer had a big force with him, was very amusing to them, considering they actually only numbered a few hundreds, and had, I think they said, two old muzzle-loading guns only with them. Having been enlisted a month before the war, they are the oldest Volunteer Force out here.

The Mails Arrive.

NEAR THE RACECOURSE,
PRETORIA.
Sunday, July 8th.

Back at the Racecourse, Pretoria. The excitement of Friday has not worn away yet. I hardly know how to describe it, especially as I must be brief, having such a lot of correspondence to get through. The men who relieved us on Friday afternoon said they had good news, and then gave it to us in these magic words: *"The mails are in!" "Thirteen bags!"* At first I could hardly believe or grasp it. The mails were in! I never expected to see a letter again. The other companies had been receiving their's for the last fortnight or more, but our whereabouts seemed unknown to the postal authorities. At last, however, we had got them. We had not had a word from our other world for over two months. It seemed over two years. The men who relieved us had come away without their's, but before we left for camp an officer, Mr. Cory, with bulging saddle-bags rode up, and they had them. We went back in the mule-waggon, and did not half exhort the nigger drivers to hurry, you can be sure. "Hi, hi! Hi-yah!! Tah!!! Nurr! *Crack-crack!!* Hamba!! Hi-yah!!!" &c. At last the ten miles were covered and our camp reached. Out of the waggon we leaped, and "Where are my letters" was the cry. Oh, the thrilling excitement of seeing the sergeant diving his hand into a sack and producing letters, papers and parcels galore. "Trooper Wilson—Wilson, Corporal Finnigan, Lance-Corporal Ross," and a big, dirty paw pounces on an envelope addressed by a well-known hand. Then another, and once again a familiar hand is recognised, then another and another. In all I had over a score of letters and about a dozen or more papers, so you can guess I have my work before me in answering them. Of course, some have been lost, especially the papers. The earliest date was April 21st, and the latest June 8th. Absolute peace and goodwill toward men reigned in our camp that night. We have all been like so many children at Christmas-time, asking one another "How many did you get?" And then on hearing the reply, probably boastfully saying, "Oh! I got more than you," and so on. It seems so pleasant to be in touch with one's world again. All the next day the fellows were poring over their letters and ever and anon, unable to suppress themselves one would be annoyed by "Ha! ha!! I say, just hear what my young sister says," or "my kiddie brother," or some such being, then an uninteresting (to other men) extract would follow.

The Nitral's Nek Disaster.

HOREN'S NEK,

NEAR PRETORIA.

Wednesday, July 11th, 1900.

(More *kopje?*)

Here I am again on the out-lying picket racket, and renewing my studies of kopjes. I am now up on them every day as well as night. When we arrived here last night, the party we relieved told us that a Russian doctor's house, about five miles out, had been raided and sacked by Boers, and no waggons were being allowed through the Nek, as the enemy were evidently waiting to catch any they could, and take them on to their commandos. Since daybreak a big action has been in progress. From the west heavy guns have been banging, and the fainter sound of volleys and pom-poming have reached our ears as we lay drowsily smoking, writing, reading and (one of us) watching on this, our observation post. In the middle of a letter to a friend a short while ago, a machine gun, apparently very close, rapped out its angry message, rat-tat-tat-tat! which startled us immensely. The whish-sh-sh of the bullets also was undoubtedly near, but as smokeless powder has usurped the place of villainous saltpetre, we failed to locate the gun, which has fired several times since.

The distant firing still continues, and as Baden-Powell is (or was) in that direction, I should imagine he is in action. It seems curious that though we are here and may at any minute be involved in the affair, yet you at home will know all about it, and we here little or nothing. But so it is.

Huge vultures, loathsome black and white birds, keep flying past us from the west. Now and again, some of them pause and circle slowly over us, as if to ascertain whether we are dead or not. A small piece of the kopje jerked at them by the most energetic member of our party, usually assures them of the negative, and with a few flaps of their wings they go whirring on. Ugh! I forgot to mention for the edification of any of our lady friends that at night rats emerge from

The Mealie & Oat Fatigue.
(What the Patriot did not altogether take into his reckoning.)

beneath the various rocks and sportively run over one's recumbent form, So, for guarding kopjes, no Amazons need apply.

Here, as "I laye a thynkynge" (to quote dear old Ingoldsby), it occurs to me that we of the Imperial Yeomanry are, in many respects, far wiser, I don't say better, men than we were six months, or even less, ago. To commence with, we know Mr. Thomas Atkins far better than we did. Now we know, and can tell our world on the best authority (*our own*) that he is the best of comrades, many of us having experienced his hospitality when in sore straits. That he will do anything and go anywhere we are certain. As regards ourselves, we have learnt to appreciate a piece of bread and a drink of water at its true worth, a thing probably none or few of us had done before—"bread and water" being usually regarded as a refreshment for the worst of gaolbirds only. And, finally, to sum our acquirements up roughly, we have learnt to shift for ourselves under any circumstances. We are hewers of wood drawers of water, cooks (though, may be, not very good ones, our resources having been limited), beasts of burden (fatigues), and exponents of many other hitherto unknown accomplishments. Allusion to fatigues reminds me of that known as "wood fatigue." It has been a usual jest of those in command to halt and bivouac us for the night at some place where there is no wood procurable, and then send us out *to get it*. Another of their little jokes has been to serve each man with his raw meat for him to cook when wood has been unobtainable. One really great result of this war already is the dearth of wood wherever the troops have been. All along the line of march, and especially where there have been halts, the wooden posts used in the construction of the various wire fencings have been chopped down or pulled up bodily and taken away, deserted houses have been denuded of all the woodwork they contained—the tin buildings collapsing in consequence. It was only a short time ago that an elderly non-combatant complained to me when I asked if he had any wood, "No, they haf take my garten fence, my best trees, and yestertay dey haf go into my Kaffir's house and commence to pull down der wood in der roof!" I am sure it is a fortunate thing that the telegraph posts are of iron. Were they wooden ones I fear stress of circumstances would have been responsible for innumerable suspensions in the telegraphic service. A scout has just been in down below with the information that we shall be attacked to-night or early to-morrow morning. The machine gun which was fired a short while ago, was one of our Colt guns at the entrance to the Nek, getting the range of a kopje opposite. These scouts (I refer to the few attached to us) are really wonderful (the battalion sergeant-major invariably alludes to them as "those d——d scouts"). Their information is always startling and mostly unreliable—still it is interesting and usually affords us vast entertainment. The scouts referred to are Afrikanders, and really chosen because they know Dutch and Kaffir. The fellows will call them interpreters, and they don't like it. On Monday I went into Pretoria to take the man of ours, who was so nearly done for in an ambush near Hatherly last month, his kit. He is now well enough to go home. He is a curious, good-natured old fellow, and in his account of the affair amused me not a little. After he had been hit and lain on the ground some time, the Boers cautiously advanced from their cover, and standing on a bank near where he laid, fired a few shots in the direction of his long-since departed comrades and then called out to him, "Hands up!" His reply, as he told me, struck me as quaint and natural, "'Ow can I 'old my 'ands up?" And seeing the reasonableness of his remark, they took his water bottle and left him where our surgeon found him. From Pretoria I have acquired quite a number of books, including half-a-dozen of Stevenson's. At present I am re-reading his "Inland Voyage."

Thursday, July 12*th.*

We were not attacked last night, although expectation ran high. We had about a thousand rounds of ammunition between the six of us, and at two o'clock in the morning had the various posts strengthened by a party of Burma Mounted Infantry (a composite corps from Burma, of Durham, Essex and West Riding Tommies). Fifteen of these were added to our small number and between us occupied four sangars at the most suitable parts of the kopje. Had we been attacked, we ought to have given a good account of ourselves, as it was a lovely moonlight night. Poor Tommy Atkins! You should have heard some of our reinforcements express themselves on the social, military, political and geographical phases of the situation. They had been rushed up from Kroonstad, and, after various vicissitudes, had been despatched to us—without rations, of course. This one wished that the By'r Lady war was over By'r Lady soon; and his next cold, hungry, tired comrade agreed with him emphatically, and consigned the whole By'r Lady country to a sort of perpetual Brock's Benefit; also the By'r Lady army, and their By'r Lady military pastors and masters, and so on. After Burma they found this country cold, especially the nights, and with them the British soldier's wish to get back to Mandalay, as expressed in the song, was a veritable fact. As usual, their experiences were worth listening to. Amongst other things, coming up from Kroonstad, they had found the burnt remains of the mails destroyed by some of De Wet's minions a little while ago (some of mine were there, I know), and had amused themselves by reading the various scraps. Some of these, they told me, were very pathetic. In one, for instance, a poor old woman had apparently sent her son a packet of chocolate, bought with her last shilling, (she was just going into the Workhouse), and she hoped that it would taste as sweet as if she had paid a sovereign for it. Had they had any mails? No, not since they had been here. They thought all their people must be dead, and "it does cheer one up to get a letter." In Burma they always give a cheer when the English mail comes in. I gave four of them some pieces of stale bread, a handful of moist sugar, and four oranges; while another of ours gave the others some bread and the remains of a tin of potted bloater. The latest news, which I believe is quite authentic, is that the remnants of the Dorset, Somerset, Devon and Sussex Yeomanry, about seventy in number, are to be remounted and attached to the 18th Hussars. This looks like more marching. I have bought, and intend bringing home with me, a few sets of the surcharged Transvaal stamps. I am doing this in a self-defensive way; my reason being that among my friends and acquaintances in the dear homeland I number certain strange beings commonly known in earlier and ruder days as stamp collectors, but now politely known and mysteriously designated *philatelists*. Now I know for a fact that these persons will, on first meeting me, demand at once, "Have you brought any sets of surcharged Transvaal stamps back?" and if I answer "Nay," what will they think of me? All the vicissitudes of the past few months, my travellings by land and water, my fastings and various little privations and experiences, will have been stupidly borne for naught in their opinion. And why? Because I have not returned laden with Transvaal stamps.

PRETORIA.

Friday, July 13*th.*

Back in camp again. At sunset, yesterday, when we came down from the observation post to get a little tea, preparatory to occupying the kopje we had been guarding at night, we found everybody on the move, and were ordered to mount and clear at once. This meant rushing up to the kopje, getting our blankets and other impedimenta, and down again, flinging them on the first horse (already saddled), and dashing away, orders having been given to abandon the post, as the Boers were in strong numbers, and between us and the town sniping. A staff-officer had told our captain that he was in charge of the valley, and wanted it to be a happy valley. We being a source of anxiety, he requested us to withdraw. I fear it had not proved a happy valley for the Lincolns and Greys, who were at Nitral's Nek, some eight miles to westward of us, and had been attacked and suffered badly in the morning. (The explanation of the heavy firing already alluded to.) Near the town we came on a broken-down ambulance waggon in a donga, out of which the wounded were being assisted as well as the circumstances permitted. Close by, on the ground, was something under a blanket, which we nearly rode over. A man close by, lighting his pipe, revealed it to us. It was one poor fellow who had died on the way. Further on, we came on numerous pickets and bivouacked troops, and men of the Lincolns and Greys at frequent intervals, asking anxiously where the ambulance waggons were, and if any of their fellows were in them. On arriving here we found our horse lines full of remounts, which looked like business. We join Mahon's Brigade on Sunday, so we are very busy looking out and cleaning up saddlery and such like.

Well, I do not feel in a letter-writing mood this morning, so shall as far as possible arrange my kit and possessions for the next move on the board, on which this poor Yeoman is a humble pawn. I have just finished the "Inland Voyage," which you may remember concludes thus, in the final chapter, "Back to the World":—

"Now we were to return like the voyager in the play, and see what re-arrangements fortune had perfected the while in our surroundings; what surprises stood ready made for us at home; and whither and how far the world had voyaged in our absence. You may paddle all day long; but it is when you come back at nightfall, and look in at the familiar room, that you find Love or Death awaiting you beside the stove; and the most beautiful adventures are not those we go to seek."

Good, isn't it?

WITH MAHON.

A General Advance to Balmoral and Back.

DASSPOORT,

OUTSIDE PRETORIA.

Tuesday, July 31st.

"Good morning! Have you used Pears' soap?" No, nor any other for about a fortnight, but in a few minutes I am going to have a most luxurious shave and bath in a tin teacup. As you can see by the above, we are all back at this historic town again after a very warm fortnight of marching and fighting under General Mahon. We marched through the town past Roberts yesterday, and are now camped awaiting remounts, in order to proceed with the game in some other and unknown direction. I have not much time for correspondence, but will do my best to give a little sketch of some of our doings. To begin with, on Saturday, July 14th, the remnants of the Dorset, Devon, Somerset and Sussex Yeomanry were formed into a composite squadron[*] of three troops under Captain Sir Elliot Lees, M.P., and served with fresh mounts—Argentines. Of course, I got a lovely beast, a black horse, which would not permit anyone to place a bit in his mouth under any circumstances. It generally takes our sergeant-major, farrier-sergeant, an officer's groom, a corporal and myself about an hour to get the aforesaid bit properly fixed. When I try to fix it myself with the assistance of a comrade, the performance usually concludes by tying him to a wheel of our ox waggon, and then, after many struggles, I manage to achieve my object all sublime (though there is not much sublimity about it). Not wanting opprobrious epithets, my steed remained nameless for the first week. I casually thought of calling

---

[*] From the first the mixture of cavalry and infantry terms used in connection with the I.Y. has been most amusing. As our officers from this date invariably referred to us in cavalry terms, the words "squadron," "troop," etc., will be used to the end of the volume.

him "Black Bess," but "he" is not a mare, and I thought it would be inappropriate. At length I struck what I consider a good name. *Bête Noire*, my *bête noire*, and so I called him, and as he is by no means averse to eating through his head rope when picketed, I find that the curtailment to "gnaw" is satisfactory enough as far as names go. Now you know something about my friend the horse, so to proceed. We moved out of our old camp on the Saturday afternoon in question, through Pretoria to another on the other side, where we joined General Mahon's crowd, amongst whom was the Imperial Light Horse, Australians, Lumsden's Horse, New Zealanders, "M" Battery R.H.A., and a squadron or so of the 18th Hussars, sometimes known as "Kruger's Own," being the captured warriors of Elandslaagte. On Sunday we had some good luck in the ration line, the 72nd and 79th Squadrons of I.Y., the Roughriders, had just come up and joined us, and had been served with innumerable delicacies, with which they did not know what to do, as they had orders that they could only take a certain quantity with them. No sooner did we hear of their embarrassment than, as the wolf swept down on the fold, we swept down upon them, and most sympathetically relieved them of tins of condensed milk, jams, and such like, and what we could not eat we managed to carry away with us for another day. On Monday our general advance commenced. It was a grand sight, after marching a few miles, to come on French's camp and see the lancers, mounted infantry and guns moving out in the early morning. A few miles on and our friend the enemy opened fire on us, or, rather, on a kopje on which we had just placed a 4.7. They sent a beautiful shot from their "Long Tom," which pitched within a few yards of where the gun had just been placed and close by Generals French and Mahon. We Mounted Infantry remained behind the kopje and dozed and lunched while desultory shells now and again whizzed over us. Beyond this, nothing occurred worth mentioning. On Tuesday morning we went out a few miles and took up a position to prevent the Boers retreating in our direction. We had to collect stones and form miniature sangars. We waited there nearly all day, during which I perused "In Memoriam," and posed for a libellous sketch done by our troop officer, entitled "An Alert Vedette." The laughter which this occasioned caused me to arise out of curiosity and ask to see the pictorial effort. The subject represented was a tramp-like being asleep behind three or four little stones. We returned in the evening to our camp and I had charge of the stable guard, an every three or four night occurrence. The next day—Wednesday, the 18th—we proceeded some miles further on, getting well into the bush country. I do not

"*Stable Guard! There's a horse loose!*"

know the name of the place we halted at for the night; it was very picturesque but had far too many kopjes (which required picketing). The next day we were off again through the bush. *Apropos* of the bush, it appears to me that every tree and shrub in this land of promise produces thorns. On Friday, the 20th, we came in touch with the enemy. We were advancing in extended order towards an innocent-looking kopje, had got close up to it, and had just dismounted, when—rap! went a Mauser. Then another. and rap, rap, rap, rap, rap, rap, and the whole show started. As there was absolutely no cover to hand, we got the order to mount and clear, which order was very promptly executed by all save one. The reports of the Mausers and the whistling buzz of the bullets startled my noble steed, *Bête Noire*, and after several ineffectual efforts to mount the brute, he broke away from me, and I, tripping over a mound as the reins slipped out of my hands, fell sprawling on my face. This, I believe, caused some of our fellows to think I was hit. Of course, after hurling a choice malediction after my horse, I was quickly on my feet and doubling after the rest of the "Boys of the Bulldog Breed." An officer of the Dorsets, Captain Kinderslie, seeing my plight, rode up amid the whistling bullets and insisted on my holding his hand and running by the side of his horse, till we came to Sergeant-Major Hunt, who had caught and was holding *Bête Noire*. Naturally, the reins were entangled in his forelegs, but I soon got them clear and mounted. Away flew my beautiful Argentine, away like the wind, every whistling, buzzing bullet seeming to help increase his bounds. At last we all got out of range, re-formed, dismounted, and advanced to attack. Soon the order was changed, and we mounted again and rode to flank the Boers, who had apparently left their first position. We reached a neighbouring kopje and halted at the base. An officer rode up, and I overheard him say that it would be advisable to send a few men in such and such a direction to find out, *with as small a loss as possible*, the position and strength of the enemy. Here it may not be out of place to mention that acting as scouts and advance parties, and drawing the fire of the enemy, has been the vocation of the Imperial Yeomanry, also of the Colonial Mounted Troops. Then four of us were ordered to ride slowly up the kopje, which was a wooded and very rocky one, and find out if any of the enemy were there. This we did. It is a peculiar feeling, not devoid of excitement, doing this sort of thing, for our horses made much noise and very slow progress over the boulders and rocks, and the possibility of a Brother Boer being behind any of the stones in front of one with a gun, of course made one reflect on the utter impossibility of shooting him or his friends, or of beating a retreat. Still, the knowledge that the report of his Mauser would warn one's comrades below was eminently satisfactory. There were no Boers there, or I should hardly be inditing this letter. They had built sangars and left them. We were posted on this kopje for the rest of the day, and at night upon another.

Our artillery had shelled them during the afternoon, and they did not trouble us again. That night we were not allowed to have any fires and our position being inaccessible to the waggons, we had no hot coffee or tea, which by the way, is one, if not the greatest, of our treats—our milkless and occasionally sugarless evening and morning coffee or tea.

On Saturday we advanced with the main body through a good deal of bush country. Sunday was one of the hardest days we had during our little fortnight's outing. We started early as advance to Ian Hamilton's Division, and during the day covered a terrific amount of ground, got well peppered on several occasions, once, during the afternoon, pushing on rather too close to the enemy, the retreating Boers gave us some warm rifle fire and then opened on us with a couple of field guns, and we had to clear. The firing was excellent. A few of us got into a bunch, and a shell whirred over our heads and struck the ground only a few yards away on our right. That day several men were killed and wounded, but none of our crowd, though one got a bullet in his rear pack, another had his bandolier struck, and another his hand grazed. The annoying part of our work was that we were repeatedly sniped at, but never had a chance to retaliate, even when we saw the enemy, as we did on several occasions. Certainly once we prepared a pretty little surprise for them in the way of an ambush formed of our troop dismounted, but they did not come. However, two or three of our fellows saw somebody by a Kaffir kraal, and thinking it was a Boer, opened fire, and whoever it was dropped. It proved only Kaffirs were there, and two men in our troop are still quarrelling as to which bagged the inoffensive nigger, if bagged he was.

Monday, the eighth day out, the entire force rested, which means in plain English that they washed, mended their clothes and performed other domestic duties. Like the man in "The Mikado," I am a thing of shreds and patches, though there is not much dreamy lullaby for me, or any of us. The next day we marched on without opposition to Bronkhorst Spruit, of fateful memory. We reached there at mid-day, and camped, as we had to wait for our convoy to come up. As soon as we had got our lines down we went to get wood—we like to have our own fires when we can. Corrugated iron buildings there were, but untenanted. Bronkhorst Spruit, of hated memory, was a deserted village. Smash!—bang!—crash!—crack! "Far flashed the red artillery," aye? No, it is merely Mr. Thomas Atkins and his brethren of the Colonies and Imperial Yeomanry, who are overcoming difficulties in the wood fatigue line. Considering that the average Transvaal house is constructed with wood and corrugated iron, it can be easily understood that neither its erection or demolition takes much time. "So mind yer eye, there—crash!—bang! That door belongs to the Sussex! Smash! Look out, the roof's coming down," etc.

The convoy came in during the night, so we were up and off at an early hour, bound for Balmoral, the next station on the line towards Middelburg. The country we had to traverse was very rough, and on our left were ranges of suspicious-looking kopjes. Soon after we started my horse funked a narrow dyke at about half-a-dozen places, and finally, on my insisting and exhorting him with my one remaining spur, plunged sideways in at the deepest part. He came out first, soaked. I followed promptly, wet to the waist (nice black water and mud); his oats and my day's biscuits, which were in his nosebag, were spoilt; and my feelings towards him none of the best. Balmoral was reached at about noon. There, I regret to state, we did not have Queen's weather. Soon after we arrived clouds began to gather, and thoughtful men commenced carrying up sheets of corrugated iron, of which there was a great quantity near the station, and hastily constructing temporary shelters. Ours was a poor concern, and as I had to wander about in the rain some time before I turned in, I was sopping wet, and of course passed the night so. Our waggon got stuck in a drift, as usual, and so we went coffee-less that night. The next day we heard that during the night an officer and three men of the Argyll and Sutherland Highlanders had died from exposure to the severe weather. On that march from Bronkhorst Spruit to Balmoral we lost hundreds of mules, oxen and horses. They simply strewed the roadsides all the way. On Friday, the 27th, we returned to Bronkhorst Spruit, *en route* for Pretoria. Leaving Bronkhorst Spruit for Pienaarspoort the next morning, we passed the graves of the massacred 94th (Connaught Rangers). First we passed three walled-in enclosures, which the officers rode up to and looked over. They were the graves of the rear guard. Then we came to a larger one, which contained the main body. The Connaughts were marching with us; whatever their feelings were, they must have felt a grim satisfaction in the knowledge that "they came again." Yesterday (Monday, July 30th,) we marched into Pretoria, past Lord Roberts, and on through the town to our present camp, which we leave at four to-morrow morning with fresh horses. We heard as we went through that one of our Sussex fellows, who was down with enteric when we left, had since succumbed. Poor fellow! It may be merely sentiment, but I must say the idea of being buried out here is somewhat repugnant to me. His bereaved relatives and friends cannot have the comforting feelings of Tennyson, expressed "In Memoriam."

> "'Tis well; 'tis something; we may stand
> Where he in English earth is laid,
> And from his ashes may be made
> The violet of his native land.
> 'Tis little; but it looks in truth
> As if the quiet bones were blest
> Among familiar names to rest,
> And in the places of his youth."

To Rustenburg.

CAMP,
TWO MARCHES WEST OF PRETORIA.
Wednesday, August 8th, 1900.

"Oh, darkies, how de heart grows weary,
Far from de ole folks at home."

There goes somebody again! It is always occurring, either vocally or instrumentally; but to start now, when I want to pull myself together and give a further account of the doings of the remnants of what was once the Sussex (69th) Squadron of Imperial Yeomanry, and their comrades of the West Countrie, is annoying beyond all expression. To commence, I must really trace out for you our bewildering descent, or ascent, to our present state, and then you will thoroughly understand why, in all probability, the papers have been silent as to the doings and whereabouts of the 69th Squadron of Imperial Yeomanry. At Maitland we belonged to the 14th Battalion of Yeomanry, under Colonel Brookfield, M.P. Leaving that salubrious but sandy locality, we travelled on our very own, by rail and road, till we joined Roberts at the Klip River, and for a few days were his bodyguard. At Johannesburg we joined the 7th Battalion of Yeomanry, under Colonel Helyar, of whose murder, in July, at a Boer's house not far from Pretoria, you must have read. Later on, men from this battalion having entered the Police and civil berths, those of us who were left were banded together and formed into one squadron under Sir Elliot Lees, M.P. This was composed of three weak troops—Dorset, Devon and Sussex, the latter troop containing half-a-dozen Somerset men. As such we left Pretoria, and went east as far as Balmoral. On our return to Pretoria, our weak horses and sick men being weeded out, we went west nearly as far as Rustenburg, as one *troop*, composed of Sussex, Devon, and Dorset men, and attached to the Fife Light Horse.* As I write, we are returning in the direction of Pretoria. And now, if you have skipped the foregoing I will proceed to give you as brief an account as possible of our adventures since leaving Pretoria a week ago (Wednesday, August 1st).

On that day, forming No. 3 Troop of the Fife Light Horse, we marched out of Dasspoort and proceeding due west, parallel with the Magaliesberg, quickly got in touch with the enemy, under Delarey, whom we slowly drove before us. Soon we came upon Horen's Nek, and the commencement of farms and orange groves. As we passed the first grove, with the glowing oranges tantalising us in a most aggravating manner, we cast longing eyes at them, but hastened on after

*This fine squadron of Yeomanry, under Captain Hodge, had also joined Mahon, at Pretoria, on July 16th.

the unfraternal Boer. The oranges were not for us—then. A little further on the fighting became warm, and we galloped up; then, "Halt! for dismounted service!" and the reins of three horses are thrown at me, or thrust into my hands by their riders, who double out to the left and proceed to participate in the fun of the firing line. Considering that I had only once (at Shorncliffe) acted as No. 3, you can picture to yourself the sort of entertainment which followed. The intelligent Argentines manœuvred round me like performing horses doing the quadrilles or an Old English Maypole dance, while with the reins we made cat's-cradles, and Gordian knots. That idiot, Mark Tapley, would indeed have envied my lot, and have been welcome to it. The row made by the firing was terrific, for pom-poms and artillery were joining in, and a fair amount of bullets came by us with the led horses. Suddenly our fellows came doubling back, and with a sigh of relief I surrendered their horses to them. Then our troop-officer, Captain Kinderslie, gave us the order, "Fours, right—Gallop!" and off we went to turn their right flank. Our course lay right across the open, and as soon as the enemy saw our move they poured their fire in as hot as they could. Round to their right we flew, with the bullets whistling by, and striking the earth before and behind us, but divil a man did they hit, though the air seemed thick with them. At last our exhilarating gallop was finished, and as our small party advanced to the attack, all they saw was the last few Boers scuttling off for dear life. Colonel Pilcher, who was with Mahon, sent round and thanked our little troop for this service.

After this we returned to an orange grove, near which our force was encamped. *That night we had oranges.*

The next day we were rear guard and, passing through a fat land, abounding with oranges, tangerines, citrons, lemons, tobacco and good water, not to forget porkers, fowls, ducks, and the like, "did ourselves proud," to resort to the vernacular. That night we had a huge veldt fire, and the whole camp had to turn out with blankets to fight it. Fortunately a well-beaten track separated the blazing veldt from us, and the wind blew it beyond, or we could hardly have made a successful stand against the flames, some being quite a dozen feet in height. Allusion to veldt fires reminds me that the last time I had to turn out to fight one was near Johannesburg, and the man who displayed most energy in smiting the flames with his blanket, and who came away from the charred veldt with blackened face and hands, was our second in command, the Duke of Norfolk.

On Friday we continued our advance, and crossed the Crocodile River. This day we saw nothing of the enemy. Our horses have done well in the way of forage lately. Sometimes we get bundles of oat hay out of the barns we visit *en route*, and strap them, with armfuls of green oats pulled from the fields, fore and aft of our saddles, till we look like fonts at harvest festivals. Thus equipped, we would form good subjects for a picture called "The Harvest Home." Yet, in spite of all the feeding they have been getting, our horses are all nearly done up.

Our present troop officer is great on the *commandeer*, and very popular. However, the other day he gave us a severe address on parade about looting, which he wound up as follows:—"Of course, I don't object to your taking the necessaries of life, such as oranges, fowls, ducks, mealie flour, or the like, but (sternly) any indiscriminate looting I shall regard as a crime."

Ambushed.

On Sunday (August 5th), while the folks at home were preparing for the Bank Holiday, we Yeomen of Sussex, Somerset, Dorset, Devon and Fife, with our friends "The Roughs," were continuing to advance west in the direction of Rustenburg. This day we passed through some of the best wooded country I have seen out here. The trees being quite large and at a distance very much like small oaks. At about mid-day we halted in front of Olifant's Nek, and our signallers tried to get into heliographic communication with the great "B.-P.," who was supposed to be in possession. At last, after several fruitless efforts, a dazzling dot in the pass appeared and commenced twinkling in response to ours.

"Twinkle, twinkle, helio,
What a lot of things you know."

Soon we received the order to advance. Then we were halted, "files about," and galloping about a mile to the rear, were drawn up, and informed that a Boer laager had been

reported under a small kopje of the Magaliesberg some
distance east from the Nek, and we were to go and
investigate the matter. The first three groups of our troop
were sent out to locate it, I being in the centre one. We
had some wretched ground to go over, and finally, without
any signs of opposition, reached the small farms lying at the
foot of the range of hills. There the left and centre group
were stopped for some considerable time by a large barbed
wire fence and, as none of us possessed any wire nippers, we
finally had to go out of our way some distance in order to
avoid it. I mention this trivial incident as illustrative of
how some Yeomanry matters of equipment have been
neglected. From my own knowledge, based on enquiry, I
find that none of the non-commissioned officers or men of
our squadron were provided with these very necessary
implements—one or two happened to have private ones, and
that is all. So much for that grumble. Now to resume.
Having overcome the barb-wire difficulty, we continued our
progress in the direction where we understood the laager
was situated, convinced in our minds that of Boers there
were none. *En route* we called at the few houses in the
neighbourhood and made slight investigations, with always
the same result. There were women and heaps of children,
but of men none. Of course, you know the game. The
chivalrous Boer, having deposited his arms in Pretoria and
taken the oath of neutrality, has rested himself, and is now
out again on the war path, either from choice or through
being commandeered. At last one of our scouts rode up
and told us that our right-hand group had found the laager
which had been evacuated. Riding through the trees, it was
rather thickly wooded, we soon came across wandering
cows, calves and oxen, and at length the laager at the foot of
a small kopje. In it were the four men of our right group,
cattle, horses, a few donkeys, and a couple of uneasy-
looking niggers, who had evidently been left behind and in
charge by the Boers. It was a fine position for a laager, and
well hidden away. Several of us dismounted here and
lighted our pipes while we watched the fine cattle we had
got, and those with bad horses haggled as to who should
possess the best of the Boer mounts, which were being held
by the uncomfortable-looking Kaffirs. Presently through

a donga on the left of the laager came the leading groups of the Fife Light Horse and soon the laager contained the first troop. I remounted my horse and—*rap!* went a shot and over rolled a horse and rider (a Sussex sergeant) on my right; then into us rapped and cracked the rifles from the near kopje. There was only one thing to do, and that was to clear. Men and horses appeared to be tumbling over on all sides, *Bête Noire* swerved and I fell off at the commencement of the fusilade. Arising, I doubled after the sergeant whose horse had been knocked over by the first shot. After going about a score of yards, I saw him dash into some bushes and brambles, and following, slipped and rolled down the side of a gully till I found myself scratched and torn sitting in a small rivulet at the bottom with my pipe still in my mouth and my rifle, the barrel of which was half choked with mud, in my hand. Looking round I saw two of our fellows who had led their horses down from the other side. The place could not have been improved on for cover, and the others falling in with my *j'y suis, j'y reste* remark, we sat down on the moist earth and rocks and awaited developments, while the bullets whistled and buzzed through the trees over our heads. Soon a volley whizzed over us from our fellows who had succeeded in retiring and rallying behind a knoll some distance back. This went on for a time, and at length the firing ceased. A Fife man came up from lower down the gully; he had lost both horse and rifle. However, crawling higher up, he found the latter in some bushes. Presently a strange figure appeared, clad in khaki, with a dark blue handkerchief tied over his head, a stick in his hand and leading a horse. This proved to be anither canny Scot. He had assumed this sort of disguise and managed to secure a horse from near the laager. He was rather apprehensive lest our own people should fire on him if they spotted him. As he told us, on our enquiring, that there were two more horses in the laager, though he advised us not to go out for them then, the Fife man and I emerged from the donga and with a wary eye on the treacherous kopjes entered the laager, which was only a score of yards from our place of concealment, and to my great delight, of the two horses quietly eating the forage there I recognised *Bête Noire* as one. Having now obtained horses, we leisurely proceeded to camp, calling on the way at a few of the farmhouses and an orange grove we had passed on our advance to the laager. The Boers had evidently cleared, or they would have fired on us as we rode to the farms in full view of the kopjes all the way. I cannot say that the simple Boer women seemed pleased to see us when we rode up with smiling faces and helped ourselves (with their permission) to oranges and tangerines, while one good lady gave me a couple of eggs, which I enjoyed later for tea. Then gaily bidding them *Auf Wiedersehen* we retraced our way and came to where the camp had been established. Arrived there, the stories we heard concerning the affair were, as you can imagine, marvellous. And, after all, what do you think the wily Boer bagged as the result of such a lovely death trap? Not a man. Half-a-dozen horses were shot, and I daresay some cattle. My rolled overcoat also had a rip suspiciously like a bullet mark. Once again Boer wiliness had been rendered ineffectual owing to execrable marksmanship. It seems like ingratitude to thus criticise their shooting, but it cannot go without comment.

On Monday, the August Bank Holiday, we did not shift camp, and had the luxury of a late *reveillé* (6 a.m.), and opportunities for very necessary washes and shaves, and such domestic duties as repairing rents in our breeches and tunics, and a little laundry work. Some of your "gentlemen rovers abroad" are finding that sewing the tears in one's tunic is a far different and more difficult matter than sowing one's wild oats at home. Owing to having baked the back of one of my boots in drying it at a fire, after my fourth immersion in a bog, I have had rather a bad heel, but am easier in that vulnerable part now, having cut out the back of the boot.

On Tuesday, B-P. very unwillingly evacuated Rustenburg, and we marched back in the direction of Pretoria.

I don't think, in spite of my verbosity, I have made any particular or direct allusion to our friend, the mule, so here I will make slight amends. Alas, he lost the little reputation he possessed at Nicholson's Nek, but to give the mule his due he is a hard worker—he has to be—he is born in bondage and dies in bondage (there is no room out here for the R.S.P.C.A.), and the golden autumn of a hard-lived life is not for the likes of him. He does not appear to get much to eat, though he will eat anything, as I found to my cost one night when in charge of the stable guard. A friend had lent me two *Graphics*, which I left on my blanket for a few minutes while I went the rounds. On my return I found a mule contentedly eating one of them—I only just managed to save half of it. When in camp, the Cape Boys, in whose charge they are, usually tie some of them to the wheels of the waggons, ammunition and water carts, the remainder being left to wander tied together in threes and fours, reminding one for all the world of Bank Holiday festivallers arm-in-arm on the so-called joyous razzle dazzle.

Out here we wandering humble builders of the Empire have no idea how the war is progressing, if progressing it is, Our noses are flat against the picture, so to speak, and, consequently, we practically see and know nothing; it is you good folks at home who have the panoramic view. Our cheerful pessimist expressed himself to this effect a few days ago. About forty or fifty years hence, travellers in this part of the world will come across bands of white-haired and silver-bearded men in strange garbs of ox and mule skin patches, and armed with obsolete weapons, wandering about in pursuit of phantasmal beings to be known in future legends as land Flying Dutchmen. Anyhow, give Private Thomas Atkins a good camp fire at night when the Army halts, round which he can comfortably sit and grumble about his rations, while he partakes of a well-cooked looted porker or fowl, and afterwards fills his pipe with the tobacco of the country, which he lights with an ember plucked from the burning, and talks of home, and the prospects, optimistic or pessimistic, of getting there some day, and at least, he is content. Oh, England, what have we not given up for thee this year, Cowes, Henley, the Derby, Ascot, Goodwood, the Royal Academy, the Paris Exhibition, the latest books and plays, all these and more—much more. And if we hadn't, what would we have done? Kicked ourselves, of course.

"Then here's to the Sons of the Widow,
Whenever, however they roam;
And all they desire, and if they require,
A speedy return to the home.
Poor beggars, they'll never see home!"

Heavy Work for the Recording Angel.

VAALBANK,
Sunday, August 12th, 1900.

I believe this place is called Vaalbank, though really I am by no means certain. Anyhow, it looks respectable to have some sort of address, so I will let it stand.

Yesterday, at Commando Nek, we were rejoined by the rest of the Composite Squadron, and remounts were brought up from Pretoria (about 300); on account of the latter I am glad that I did not commence this letter the same evening, for we Yeomanry had to lead them. The brutes were Hungarians and Argentines. Niggers had brought them from Pretoria, and then we had to take them on, while the men in need of horses toiled along on foot. Why they were not allotted on the day they were received is only accounted for by the fact of our forming part of a British Army. During the "telling-off" of our fellows to the various groups of sorry nags, a comrade known as "Ed'ard" and I loafed in rear of the squadron in hopes of coming last and finding no horses left. We did come last, but there being eleven horses over, poor Ed'ard had six and I five Argentines to lead, and the Recording Angel had a big job on. Half-a-dozen rapid type-writers on his staff would have failed to cope with the entries entailed by that day's work and discomfort. Some people boast that they can be led, but not driven. The boast of my Argentines was that they could be driven but not led. For about three hours I led, or tried to lead them, at the end of which time my right, or leading arm, was about four inches longer than my left, and once or twice quite six. This was when a ditch or some such obstacle had to be overcome. My own steed, having nobly negotiated it, two of the others would follow his excellent example, and then the remaining three would pause on the bank, irresolutely at first, and then quite determined not to "follow my lead," in fact to never "follow me," would pull back a bit. Then a lovely scramble would result, in which I would be hauled half-way back, horse and all, and my rifle, instead of remaining properly slung, would become excitable, and manage to hang round my neck or waist. Finally a fairy godmother, in the form of a dirty, unshaven Tommy Atkins

44   A YEOMAN'S LETTERS.

of the line, would come to my assistance, and with a wave of his wand—I mean rifle—and a thrust with the butt, my troubles for the moment would be overcome. At last, with my right hand cut and sore, and a temper which would have set the Thames afire, I let go the leathern thong by which I had been endeavouring to lead them, and started driving

A terrible reckoning!
Binks (who has just had a row with a bugle Sergeant and got an extra stable guard, is also 'forit'): "By Heavens! Wait till I get home and meet him in civvies, and he has no stripes to protect him!"

them. Other fellows also commenced to do the same, and after the brutes we raced, inhaling dust, expectorating mud, and cursed by every transport officer. Happy men, without horses to look after, were looting fowls and porkers, for the district was a good one; but such was not for us luckless Yeomen. Even when we got into camp we had to stand for nearly two hours in the dark, looking after the brutes till some more Yeomanry, the Roughs, relieved us, I cannot help it—it's the twelfth, and I must *grouse!*

Listen to this! When at home in barracks, and on the transport, the orderly officer always went through the army routine of going round at meals and asking "Any complaints?" Now that we are campaigning, divil an officer asks if we have any complaints to make, or is in any way solicitous as to our welfare or wants. And the consequence is this: we are at the mercy of our quartermaster-sergeants, who are sometimes fools, and more often the other thing as far as we are concerned, and beings known by us as "the waggon crowd," *i.e.:* the cooks, and divers other non-combatants. What they don't want, or dare not withhold, is given to the poor Yeoman, who has to march, fight, and do pickets and guards. The man who marches and fights is the worst paid and worst treated out here. This, it appears, is a way they have in the army. It is, however, distinctly amusing to hear the *common* troopers proclaiming how they will get equal with their officers, especially the non-coms., when they meet them in the sweet by-and-bye as civilians.

The night we stopped outside Pretoria before coming out this way, our curiosity was aroused by suddenly hearing three hearty British cheers from some lines not far from ours. On making an enquiry as to the cause of this outburst of feeling, we were informed that the battalion had just received the news that their adjutant, who was absent on leave, had been made a prisoner by the Boers. Of course, some officers, especially the Regular ones who have seen previous service, are decidedly popular, our present General—"Mickey" Mahon—being an instance. There is no gold lace or cocked hat about him. He is, in attire, probably the strangest figure in the campaign. Picture to yourself a square-built man of middle age, wearing an ordinary brown cap (not a service one), a khaki coat with an odd sleeve, breeches, and box-cloth gaiters, carrying a hooked cherrywood stick, and smoking a briar, and you have General Mahon.

And now listen to this little story about him. A few days ago a Tommy was chasing a chicken near a farm on the line of march. Suddenly the cackling, fluttering, feathered one dashed in the direction of a plainly-dressed stranger. "Go it, mate; you've got 'un!" yelled the excited Tommy. Then, to his horror, he recognised the general, and, confused, tried to apologise. "Not at all," said the chief, and helped him to kill the bird. Then telling him if he liked he could take it to his colonel and say the general had helped him to kill it, he sauntered away.

His favourite corps is the I.L.H., and he seems quite pained when they miss an opportunity of obtaining good loot, which, once or twice they have done, owing to a stringent order from someone else against it.

Routine and red tape, though probably not so bad as "once upon a time," are still rampant, and we Yeomanry get our full share of them, the Colonials being more exempt. When we are on the march it is always "dress up there" or back as the case may be, and the following extract from a comrade's diary can be regarded as absolutely veracious.

"August 6th. On advance party again. Tried to look for Boers and lost my 'dressing.' Severely reprimanded."

It appears to me that our way for locating the enemy is absurdly simple. We advance in approved extended order, so many horses' lengths, not more nor less, if any Boers are about, and we get too close to them, they pot at us. Then we take cover, if not bowled over; and it is generally known that there are Boers about.

This (Sunday) morning, I am writing a few lines during a halt—we passed various farms on our way, which is in the direction of Krugersdorp. We are in hopes of rounding up De Wet (don't laugh!) At one of these farms, as we passed, a regular old Rip Van Winkle Dopper Boer was seated by his door scowling at us, and a trooper who had evidently been sent to ask for arms presently received, and rode away with *a sword*. It was really most amusing, probably the dear old man had three Mausers under his floor boards, and perhaps a bathchair was to be found somewhere on the premises, in which he could be conveyed to the top of a kopje now and again, to enjoy the pleasure of sniping the *verdommte Rooineks*, or their convoy as it passed along.

Monday, August 13th. On this day we made a reconnaissance in force, but had no fighting. In the evening we had to do an outlying picket on a near kopje, some long range and ineffective sniping going on as we took up our position at sunset. The waggon having been left behind (no unusual occurrence), we went tea-less to our night duty.

Tuesday, August 14th. Off, without any coffee, on advance guard. As we moved out of camp, revolvers and rifles were banging in all directions. However, it was not sniping, but merely the usual killing of sick horses and mules. Along the road the defunct quadrupeds hummed dreadfully (if any tune, "The place where the old horse died").

Relief of Eland's River Garrison. Join in the great De Wet hunt.

Wednesday, August 15th (in the vicinity of Eland's River). Another day without tea or coffee, and in a district lacking in wood and water. At about mid-day we came upon Kitchener, Methuen, and others with their respective forces. Colonel Hore's gallant Australians and Rhodesians had just been relieved. The various columns halted and camped here. That afternoon a couple of commandeered sheep were served out to our troop; I dressed one, and obtained the butcher's perquisites, viz.: the heart, liver and kidneys. On these, with the addition of a chop from a pig, at whose dying moments I was present, and a portion of an unfortunate duck, I made an excellent meal. That night was rather an uneasy one for me, for I had Eugene-Aram-like dreams in which relentless sheep chased me round farmhouses and barns into the arms of fierce ducks and avenging porkers. But *reveillé*, and then daylight came at last, and peace for my burdened mind and chest.

Thursday, August 16th. Off in the direction of Olifant's Nek. At noon we came in contact with the scouts of the enemy who were holding the Nek. After being under a heavy rifle fire, we retired to camp and waited for the morrow. Ian Hamilton arrived in the evening with his infantry and cow-guns.

Friday, August 17th. We moved out early in anticipation of a big day, for amongst the various rumours was one to the effect that De Wet's laager was on the other side of the Nek, and Baden-Powell and Methuen were going to attack him from that quarter. Oh, the rumours about this slim individual, they are legion! Here are some of the hardy perennial order:

1. De Wet is captured at last.
2. De Wet is surrounded and cannot escape. (The modification brand.)
3. De Wet has escaped with eleven men.
4. De Wet has 4,000 men with him.
5. De Wet has only 300 men with him.
6. De Wet has heaps of stores and ammunition.
7. De Wet has no stores, etc.

This is supposed to be the dry season, but it appears to me to be De Wet, and our "Little British Army which goes such a very long way" (quite true especially here) seems like the British Police, who always have a clue, and expect shortly to make an important arrest, but don't. We took up a position on a kopje opposite to the right of the Nek, and for a few hours had a rare easy time. Divesting ourselves of our tunics, belts, bandoliers and other top hamper, we lounged about in our shirt-sleeves, smoking and dozing, only rousing ourselves a bit later when the double-rapping reports of the Mausers over the way told us that our scouts were being fired on. Soon the R.H.A. came into action, and were quickly followed by the banging of the cow-guns. It was most interesting to see where the shells struck, and how soon the kopjes and Nek opposite became blackened, smoking rock and earth, and the spiteful Mausers ceased from troubling. Meanwhile, the infantry, Berks and A. and S. Highlanders, advanced and the Nek was ours, and the Boers, De Wet's rearguard—vamoosed. Then we all marched through the Nek, which was a wonderful position, and possible of being held after the manner of Thermopolæ. Our Sussex farrier-sergeant was shot in the arm. Going through the Nek we passed three graves by the roadside—graves of Royal Fusiliers who had died of wounds and enteric during B.-P.'s occupation of the place a short time previous. A soldier's grave out here is a simple matter, a rude cross of wood made from a biscuit case, with a roughly-carved name, or perhaps merely a little pile of stones, and that is all, save that far away one heart at least is aching dully and finds but empty solace in the *pro patria* sentiment. When one passes these silent reminders of the possibilities of war, it is impossible to suppress the thought "It might have been me!" But more often than not any such morbid reflections are effaced by the sight of a house and the chances of loot. Which reminds me that we ravaged with fire and sword a good deal in the vicinity of Rustenburg, numerous houses being set afire by authority—in most cases the reason being because the owner of the domicile had broken his oath of allegiance and was out again fighting us. We reached Rustenburg at about six o'clock, and had to go on outlying picket on a terribly-high kopje, known as Flag Staff Hill, at once. So just as it became dark—tired and tea-less, with overcoats and bundles of blankets—a little band of wearied, cussing Empire builders set out on their solitary vigil, with none of your "Won't-come-home-till-morning" jollity about them. Oh, that thrice, nay seventy-times-seven, execrated hill! Up it we stumbled with a compulsory Excelsior motto, staggering, perspiring profusely, with wrenched ankles, cut and sore feet, cussing when breath permitted, dropping exhausted, and resting now and again. Thus we ascended Flag Staff Hill. On the top we found strong sangars with shell-proof shelters, which had been built by the indefatigable Baden-Powell during his occupation of Rustenburg. That night passed at last.

After De Wet.

Saturday, 18th August. We set off again in the direction of Pretoria, and unsaddled and formed our lines at about four, and were congratulating ourselves on getting camped so soon when the faint but unmistakable cry of "saddle up" was heard afar off, then nearer and nearer, till we got it. De Wet (thrice magic name) was not very far off, and we were to push on at once after him. So off we set on a forced night march, on which no lights were allowed, and mysterious halts occurred, when we flung ourselves down at our horses' feet on the dusty road and took snatches of sleep. Then a rumbling would be heard, and down the column would come the whisper "The guns are up"—probably some obstacle such as a drift or donga had delayed them—then forward. We halted at twelve and were up again at four. The day being Sunday we, as usual out here, rested not, but proceeded on the warpath. A few miles down the road a scout passed with a Boer prisoner (Hurrah! one Boer less!). Leaving the Pretoria road soon after daybreak, we made for some low-lying ranges of hills, known as the Zwart Kopjes, and after going forward a couple of miles our guns, M Battery, trotted smartly forward in line, halted, then like wasps cut off at the waists, the fore parts flew away leaving the stings behind. In plain military words, the R.H.A. unlimbered, busy gunners laid their pets, others ran back for ammunition, an officer gave directions, then a roll of smoke, a flash, a cracking bang, a gun runs back, and intently-watching eyes presently see a small cloud of smoke over the top of a distant kopje, and a faint, far-away crack announces that the well-timed shrapnel is searching the rocky ridges; then bang, bang! bang, bang! and the rest quickly follow, firing in turn and now and again in twos or threes. Then it's "limber up" and forward, and their attention is paid to another little range further on. Soon, having cleared several kopjes, we, the Fife Light Horse, New Zealanders, our Composite Squadron, and others, crossed a drift and leisurely advanced, passing on our way a deserted Boer waggon loaded with corn, mealies and other stuff. At a farmhouse we naturally managed to halt, and tried to secure edibles. Colonel Pilcher, however, came and ordered us to form up in a field further on, and as we proceeded to obey this order, Mausers began rapping out at us from a range of hills which we had supposed (usual fallacy!) were unoccupied, our guns having shelled them well. Thereupon the colonel immediately told us to retire behind the farmhouse and outbuildings with the horses. I soon found myself lying behind a low bank with Lieutenant Stanley, of the Somerset Yeomanry, on one side of me and a New Zealander the other, blazing away in response to B'rer Boer opposite. My Colonial neighbour's carbine got jammed somehow or other, and his disgust was expressed in true military style, for the keenness of the New Zealander is wonderful. One of our pom-poms and M Battery joining in, after a time the firing slackened, and chancing to look round at the side of the farmhouse, I beheld two of our fellows helping themselves to some chicken from a three-legged iron pot over a smouldering fire. Thereupon, I promptly quitted the firing line, and joined in the unexpected meal. It was awfully good, I assure you. While finishing the fowl, a New Zealander, pale-faced, with a wound in his throat and another in his hand, was brought in by two comrades, and a horse, which had been shot, died within a few yards of us. I am sorry to say that in this little affair we lost an officer and a trooper killed, and several wounded, not to mention a considerable amount of killed and wounded horses.

The next day we advanced under a heavy fire from our guns, but met with no opposition. Our objective this time was the Zoutpan District, which is principally composed of bush veldt.

Here I must pause, and give a veracious account of a certain not uninteresting episode, which happened during our march after De Wet in the Zoutpan District, and which I will call

The Yeoman, the Argentine and the Farrier-Sergeant.

On Tuesday, August the 22nd, we were advance guard through the bush veldt, and shortly after starting, *Bête Noire*, who had gradually been failing, gave out, so behold me, alone to all intents and purposes, bushed. Of course I immediately took careful bearings, and assuming that we should not be changing direction, slowly marched straight ahead. After going a considerable distance I got on to a small track, and finally, what might be termed by courtesy, a road, and was carefully studying it when one of our sergeants and a staff officer rode up. I told the latter that my horse was done, and the noble steed bore out my statement by collapsing under me as I spoke. The officer advised me to wait for the main body and lead my horse on after them, which I did, dragging him along for about a dozen weary miles, till I reached the camp at dark, just in time to participate in a lovely out-lying picket. The next morning, having reported the case to the sergeant-major, he told me to lead the horse from the camp with the convoy, and instructed the farrier-sergeant to shoot him a little way out. So, having put my saddle on our waggon and asked the farrier if he had been told about the shooting, I proceeded to drag the poor beggar along. After toiling forward some considerable distance, I looked around for the man whose duty it was to shoot him, but could see him nowhere. So on I pushed, inquiring of everybody, "Where

Some of the pomp & circumstance of Glorious War.

is the Farrier-Sergeant?" I lagged behind for him, and then toiled, perspiring and ankle deep in dust, ahead for him, but found him not. Even during the mid-day halt I could not find him, and as the beast had fallen once, I was getting sick of it. Everybody I accosted advised me to shoot the brute myself, the same as other fellows did in most of the Colonial corps, so at length, to cut this part of the story short, giving up all hope of being relieved of my burden by the farrier-sergeant, who somewhere was ambling along comfortably on a good horse—having again had the sorry steed fall—I led him aside from the track of the convoy and ended his South African career with my revolver. Alas, *Bête Noire!* Had we but understood one another better the parting would have been a sad one. The case being otherwise, I felt, it must be admitted, no regret whatever. And now the interesting part of the episode begins. Hearing my shots (I am sorry to say I fired more than once in accomplishing my fell deed) the farrier-sergeant galloped up. "Who gave you permission to shoot this horse?" "Nobody; I couldn't find you, and couldn't lug the brute any further." "I shall report you." "I don't care." Then followed high words, involving bitter personalities and we parted. After tramping a good dozen miles further, I arrived at our camp in the dark, and had the luck to find our lines soon. To an interested and sympathetic group of comrades I related in full my adventures. Our sergeant-major, who is a very good sort, was telling me that it would be all right, when the regimental sergeant-major came up and told me that he must put me under arrest for shooting my horse without permission, destroying Government property (Article 301754, Par. 703, or something like that). There was none of the pomp about the affair which I should have liked to see— no chains, no fixed bayonets, or loaded rifles. Our sergeant-major, without even removing his pipe, said "Ross, you are a prisoner," and I replied "Righto," and proceeded to inquire when the autocrats of the cook-house would have tea ready. A few days later, I was brought before the beak— the officer in command of our squadron. "Quick march. Halt, left turn. Salute." This being done, the case was stated. The farrier-sergeant told the requisite number of lies. I denied them, but of course admitted shooting the beggar. Dirty, unwashed, unkempt, unshaven, ragged wretch that I looked, I daresay on a charge of double-murder, bigamy and suicide, I should have fared ill. The captain gave me what I suppose was a severe reprimand, told me that probably in Pretoria I should have to pay something, and said he would have to take away my stripe, so down it went, "reduced to the ranks." "Salute! Right turn," etc. Thus, did your humble servant lose the Field Marshal's bâton which he had so long been carrying in his haversack. Alas, how are the mighty fallen! Tell it in Hastings and whisper it in St. Leonards if you will, like that dear old reprobate Mulvaney, "I was a corp'ril wanst, but aftherwards I was rejooced," *Vive l'Armée! Vive la Yeomanrie!* All the fellows were intensely sympathetic, and indeed, one or two particular friends seemed far more aggrieved than myself. I ripped off my stripe at once, and tossed it in our bivouac fire, and joined the small legion of ex-lance corporals of the Sussex Squadron (five in number).

"Or ever the blooming war was done,
Or I had ceased to roam;
I was a slave in Africa,
And you were a toff at home."

Hullo! When it comes to poetry it is time to conclude.

P.S.—My costume is holier than ever. Still, I find every cloud has a silver lining (though my garments possess none of any kind, unfortunately). The great advantage of the present state of one's clothes is this, if you want to scratch yourself—and out here on the warpath one occasionally does—say it's your arm, you need not trouble to take your tunic off; you simply put your hand through the nearest hole or rent, and there you are; if it's your leg you do the same, and thus a lot of trouble is saved.

Commandeering by Order.

NEAR THE RACECOURSE,
PRETORIA.

Friday, August 31st, 1900.

We arrived here on Tuesday last (28th), and since then have been camped almost on the very spot where we were in June, and are expecting every moment to receive further marching orders. These we should undoubtedly have got long ere now, if we had only obtained remounts, which are very scarce. General Mahon has gone on to Balmoral with the I.L.H., Lumsden's Horse, and other corps with horses, and this morning Colonel Pilcher paraded us, New Zealanders, Queenslanders and I.Y., and bade us good-bye. He has been connected with the Colonials from the beginning of the campaign, and took the Zealanders into their first fight. I am feeling awfully fagged to-day, so hope you will, in reading this letter, make allowance for extenuating circumstances. If you only knew, I think you do, what these letters mean, the self-denied slumbers and washes, *fatigues shirked*, books and papers unread, and other little treats which comrades have indulged in when the rare and short opportunities have occurred—you would forgive much. On Tuesday (August 21st) we had five Sussex men and three Somerset in the ranks of our troop of the Composite Squadron of Yeomanry, the rest being either in the ambulances or leading done (not "dun") horses with the waggons. In this district we came across numerous Kaffir villages, from which we drew mealies and handed in acknowledgments for the same payable in Pretoria. Reference to these papers reminds me that some of the Colonials in commandeering horses from peaceful Boer farmers have given them extraordinary documents to hand in to the authorities at Pretoria. For instance, one paper would contain the statement that Major Nevercomeback had obtained a roan mare from Mr. Viljoen Botha, for which he agreed to pay him £20, others of which I have heard and since forgotten were intensely amusing. On Wednesday (the 22nd) I had to do a footslog, owing to my horse giving out. Later I shot him, but I have made a special reference to this tragic event and its sequence already. That day we did about 25 miles through the bush veldt bearing about N.W. On the line of march not a drop of water was to be got. Though thirst is by no means a new experience, it is always a disagreeable one. On we trudged with dry, parched mouths and lips sticking together as though gummed, the dust adhering to our perspiring faces and filling our nostrils and ears. It is quaint to note how little on the march men converse with one another. On they stolidly tramp or ride hour after hour, side by side, and often exchange never a word. On they go, thinking, thinking, thinking. It is not hard to guess each other's thoughts, because we know our own. They are of home, home, home, nine times out of ten. At dark we reached our camp, and from the water-cart, for which we all, as usual, rushed, we filled our pannikins and bottles with water, thick, soapy-looking water, but to us, cool, refreshing nectar.

Thursday (the 23rd). There was a rumour (there always is) that we were to return to Pretoria. But the direction we took on marching belied it. Of course, I was "footslogging," but this day, having no horse to drag after me, was able to wander more at leisure. A few miles on the way a comrade and myself found a lovely flowing stream of the thick water before alluded to. Here we had a grand wash, and refilling our water bottles set on our journey refreshed. Some miles further on we came upon a freshly-deserted Boer store and farmhouse. Near the house we found some clips of explosive Mauser cartridges which had been buried by some bushes, and probably unearthed by some of the wandering porkers in the neighbourhood. Said I to a Tommy of Hamilton's column, as I took a handful of cartridges, "These will do as curios." Quoth Thomas scornfully, "Curios be blowed, put 'em in the beggars!" Of course, you can guess he did not exactly use those identical words, but they will do. Then having joined in the destruction of a monster hog, and obtained my share of his inanimate form, I, triumphant and perspiring, continued to follow the convoy.

Friday (the 24th). This day we expected a big fight, but, as usual, because it was expected, it did not come off. Baden-Powell the day before had hustled them pretty considerably. We were so close on the Boers, that we got half of their ambulances, one being a French presentation affair, and driven by a woman, also some waggons. This day we did not go very far, our objective being a place known, I believe, as Warm Baths (the Harrogate or Sanatorium of the Transvaal). It lies due north of Pretoria, and about 40 miles from Pietersburg. Of course, here we struck the railway. After picketing the horses, a sick sergeant's horse was handed over to me. Most of us got permission to go and get a wash. The place was empty—save for some of Baden-Powell's men, who had got in at the enemy the day before—a desolate, wind-swept, sandy plain on the edge of the bush veldt and at the base of a range of kopjes, comprised of about thirty large corrugated iron bath houses (each containing two bath rooms), a fairly large hotel and small station—such is Warm Baths. The baths were well patronised. Some of our fellows, prisoners the Boers had been obliged to leave behind in their flight—the rogues had taken the linchpins out of some of the Boer waggon wheels to impede them as much as possible—were using them as sleeping apartments. As about a score of men were after each bath and the doors had no bolts, a bath, though luxurious, was not an altogether private affair, the person bathing having continually to answer the question of a string of "the great unwashed," "How long shall you be?" and having the uneasy knowledge that about half-a-dozen impatient beings were waiting, sitting on the door-step and exhorting him "to buck up!" A couple of us managed to secure a fine bath, which we enjoyed without interruption worthy of mention. The water, which is naturally hot, was grand, and so hot that we had to use a lot of the cold, which was also laid on.

The next day, Saturday (25th), we rested at Warm Baths, and I think we deserved it. If "early to bed and early to rise, make a man healthy, wealthy and wise," excepting occasionally the first clause "early to bed," I consider we ought all to live the health and longevity of Methuselah or Old Parr, the wealth of Crœsus or Vanderbilt, and the wisdom of Solomon, blended with the guile of the Serpent. Mention of the guile reminds me of a simple little incident which occurred to-day, and which, months ago, we simple Yeomen would never have perpetrated. A terrible thing happened during the night; the sergeant-major's horse had got loose from our lines and was missing. Down came that indignant officer and sent the whole troop out to find it. Months ago I should have gone and searched diligently, and then been cussed for not finding the animal. But now, what does the fully-fledged Imperial Yeoman do? Grumbling and scowling (you must always do this, as it shows how successful the powers have been in delegating a distasteful task to you, and pleases them accordingly) with razor, soap and shaving brush in my pocket, and a growling, sullen comrade with a towel and sponge in his, we two set out in search of the noble steed. However, once out of sight, we hied us down to some running water, where we shaved and washed, then, filling our pipes, we sat down for an hour and chatted. Finally, we returned disconsolate and horseless, only to find that the great man had found it himself.

58   A YEOMAN'S LETTERS.

Sunday (26th). We got definite orders to march to Pretoria, the sick and horseless men having left by rail the previous day in trucks drawn by bullocks, till they could get on a more unbroken line. We paraded at 3 o'clock, and very

The Government has got to strike the happy medium in the sizes of the uniforms etc. which it provides for its troops

shortly after starting my new horse became bad and I had to again join the convoy. To-day we marched to Pienaars

River, the bridge here representing a badly-made switchback railway, and those marvels of energy, the Engineers, working away merrily at it, with the assistance of Kaffirs.

On Monday (27th) our *reveille* was at five, and we marched to Waterval, where we saw the fine, large aviary in which the Boers kept the British prisoners till June, and the next day (Tuesday) we were up at 2.30, and marched into Pretoria and camped on the Racecourse at 11 o'clock. No sooner had I dragged my horse in and picketed him in our lines, than I managed to obtain town leave, and, having hastily washed, I boarded a mule waggon and was soon jolted into Pretoria. There I got Mails galore, found my kit bag had come up from Cape Town, and met dozens of old comrades in the Police, who insisted on making me have tea with them (with *condensed milk* in it, oh, ye gods!) and jam on real *bread*, and generally made a fuss of me, and listened with amused attention to a truthful account of the death of *Bête Noire* and my subsequent Dreyfus-like degradation. Rattling good fellows they were to me, and under their benign influence the petty trials and inconveniences of the past seven or eight weeks faded away like a dissolving view. The authorities have also served us out with clothes. I have received a lovely khaki tunic with beautiful brass buttons stamped with Lion and Unicorn, "*Dieu et mon Droit*," and a' that. And the fit is a wonderful fit; it is truly marvellous how they can turn out such a well-fitting coat for—a big boy of twelve. And I have boots! A grand fit for a policeman. Only I am neither a boy of twelve nor a policeman.

WITH CLEMENTS.

HEKPOORT,
September 5th, 1900.

We've stood to our nags (confound them!)
   We've thought of our native land;
We have cussed our English brother,
   (For he does not understand.)
We've cussed the whole of creation,
   And the cross swings low for the morn,
Last straw (and by stern obligation)
   To the Empire's load we've borne.

Monday, September 3rd. *Reveillé* at three o'clock, and coming after a few days of welcome rest in the camp by the Pretoria Racecourse, a camp resembling a vast rubbish field with the addition of open latrines, we naturally felt more annoyed than when on the march, hence these idle rhymes. On Sunday, after a short Divine Service, at which our major presided, we had to fall in and draw remounts. Hence "Reveillé," "Saddle up and stand to your horses!" I chose rather a good mount in the horse corral, but as the sergeants had the privilege of choosing from those we drew, I lost it, and so abandoned any intentions of trying to secure another good one. There is no attempt on these occasions to see that the right man has the right horse: it's "Hobson's choice." Even at Maitland camp, where I drew my first mount, no such attempt was made, the consequence being that I, scaling about 13-st. or more with my kit on, and heaven only knows what with my loaded saddle, drew when my turn came a weak little mare, which I had to stick to, to our mutual disadvantage, while lighter men drew bigger and stronger horses. Only a few days ago I received amongst my mails a letter from my sister, who inquired, "How is your horse?" Which one? "Stumbles" is not, "Ponto" is not, "Juggernaut" is not, "Diamond Jubilee" is not, "Bête Noire" is not. My present one, which I have not named, *is*, and I sometimes wish he wasn't. When

I drew him at a venture, I vainly hoped he was not like other horses, especially that Argentine. Well, apart from stumbling and reverentially kneeling on most inopportune occasions, I have not much fault to find with him. To-day is our first day on this fresh jaunt (we are to join Clements), and already more than half the horses dished out to us seem played out. You see they have all passed through the Sick Horse Farm, and I presume are really convalescents. They dragged us along at the commencement of the day, and we had to drag them along at the end, which may sound like an equal division of labour, but which, in my opinion, it is not. However, to be very serious, our lives might have to depend upon these brutes at any moment, apart from the fact of our necks being perpetually in danger on account of their stumbling propensities. Still apart from the inconvenience of having to bury one, I fancy there would not be much concern on that count. We have halted at Reitfontein which is a mile or so from Commando Nek. Here is a large A.S.C. depôt, from which columns working in the district can draw supplies. It has been quite a treat to have tea by daylight.

Tuesday, September 4th. 'Nother three o'clock *reveillé!* Passing by Commando Nek we were surprised at the difference since we were here about a month ago. Then the trees were bare, nearly all the veldt burnt and black, and the oat fields trodden down. Now the trees are wearing o' the green, and the once blackened veldt has assumed a verdant and youthful appearance, while the oat fields remind one of home, almost. For this is the Krugersdorp District, which we like so well, though, alas, the orange groves are on the other side (north) of the Magaliesberg. A strange thing happened after passing our old camping ground (of about a month ago) at Commando Nek. Instead of recognising familiar landmarks and houses, everything seemed strange and new to me. Said the man on my left in the ranks, "There's the farm where those Tommies got the porkers." To which I remarked vacantly, "Oh!" Then, further on, "Haven't the oats come on in that field?" Again, I helplessly "Er—yes." Then, "I wonder if they've got any fowls left in that shanty over there?" I, dissembling knowledge no longer, at last observed, "Really I don't understand it. I can't remember this place a bit." To which my neighbour replied, "Don't you remember coming this way when we were leading those Argentine remounts?"

Those Argentine remounts! All was explained at last. Of course, I saw and remembered naught save those awful brutes.

We caught Clements up at ten o'clock—encamped to our joy—so here we are with "piled arms," "saddles off," and "horses picketed." As we came into camp we heard once again the Mausers of the snipers afar off. We have rigged up a sun shelter and have just dined, our "scoff" (Kaffir for "grub") being bread and bully beef.

Apropos:
First Yeoman: "I say, is this bully beef American?"
Second Yeoman: "No, '*Orse*-tralian, I believe."

Wednesday, September 5th.
> "The peaches are a-blooming,
> And the guns are a-booming,
> And I want you, my honey,
> *Yus, I do.*"

We had *reveillé* at a more Christian-like time this morning (4.30), and moved out as supports to our other troop (Devons), who were advance party. We number eighteen Sussex men, all told, in our ranks, and are led by Mr. Stanley, a Somerset I.Y. officer, who on our last trip was in charge of the Ross Gun Section, which consisted of two quick-firing Colt guns. After bare trees, dry veldt and dusty tracks, it is a real treat for one's eyes to see this fine district assuming its spring garb. Through the bright green patches of oats and barley we rode, past peach trees and bushes in full bloom, sometimes through a hedge of them, the pink blooms brushing against one's cheek. Then we came to a bend of the Crocodile River, with its rugged banks covered with trees and undergrowth, and the water rushing swiftly along between and over the huge rocks in its bed. This we forded at the nearest drift, the water reaching up to the horses' bellies. The general idea was for us mounted troops to clear the valley, and the infantry the ridges of kopjes. We were soon being sniped at from the right and the left, by, I presume, numerous small parties of Boers, and after riding about a mile were dismounted behind a farmhouse, and took up a position on the banks of the Crocodile. The scene was truly idyllic. Below us the river in this particular place was placidly flowing, the various trees on its banks were bursting out in their spring foliage, and birds were twittering amongst them : indeed, one cheeky little feathered thing came and perched on a peach tree covered in pink blossom close by and piped a matin to me, and there was I, lounging luxuriously in the deep grass, a pipe in my mouth, a Lee-Enfield across my knees, and a keen eye on the range of kopjes opposite. Truly, the spring poet's opportunity, but alas, beyond the few lines with which I have dared to head to-day's notes, I could do naught in that line. Soon our artillery began throwing shrapnel on the top of the objectionable height, and, later, the Mausers began to speak a little further on, and that has been the day's game. I don't know our losses yet, but we have undoubtedly had some. Our crowd had a horse killed, of course. We had a good deal of visiting to do, calling at this farm and that, and inquiring if the "good man" was at home. This is the usual scene:

Farmhouse of a humble order. A few timid Kaffirs loitering around, also a few fowls and slack-looking mongrels. Gentleman in Khaki rides up, and in the door appear two or more round-faced women wearing headgear of the baby-bonnet mode, dirty-faced children in background.

G. in K. : "Where is your husband?"

Women : "Niet verstand."

G. in K. : "Where is your brother?"

Women : "Niet verstand."

G. in K. : "Is he on those kopjes, potting at us?"

Women : "Niet verstand."

G. in K. : "Have many Boers been past here?"

Women : "Niet verstand."

G. in K. (After more interrogatories and more "Niet verstands") : "Oh, hang it, good-bye."

Women (in distance) : "Niet verstand."

Verily, the "niet verstand" or "no savvee" game is a great one out here.

(Later.) Our casualties were three Northumberland Fusiliers killed and eight wounded, one of our Fife comrades shot in the chest, also three Roughriders hit, and a fair percentage of horses knocked.

Thursday, September 6th.—*Reveillé* at four o'clock, and off at daybreak. We soon came into action, some of our fellows on the right flank getting it particularly hot. Our little lot wheeled and dismounted behind a farmhouse, and, wading through a field of waving green barley, under fire, took up a position amongst the growth on the near bank of the river, from which we let off at some sangars on the top of a kopje in front. After a while we returned to our horses, mounted, rode away to our right, crossed the river, dismounted behind a rise in the ground, and proceeded to occupy some kopjes nearer the enemy, who had retired. Some fine sangars were on the hill we occupied, and so we were saved the trouble of building any. The one I found myself in was a very comfortable and secure affair as regards rifle fire. As, of course, Mr. Boer does not show himself over much, we had not much to pot at, therefore I made myself as comfortable as possible on the shady side of the sangar, and pulled out one of my numerous pocket editions of Tennyson (recently acquired in Pretoria) and indulged in a good, though occasionally interrupted, read. To a stranger at the game, I should imagine that my behaviour at times would have appeared incongruous, for while perusing the "Lotos-Eaters" and "Choric Song," the man on my right would now and again interrupt me with, "There are some, have a shot at 'em!" Whereupon I would arise and fire a round or so at the distant dots, and then sink down again and resume the sweet poesy, ignoring as much as possible the constant bangings of villainous cordite in my ears, right and left. Soon we moved on to another position, the Northumberlands taking up our old one. The next one was in a stone enclosure, which contained a large number of goats and kids. This was not so pleasant, as the sun was high, and the place odoriferous.

At about three we were relieved by a Northumberland picket, and returned under a sniping fire to where the camp had been pitched. Then the fun commenced. A rather distant bang, *whis-sh!* over our heads; and from amongst the infantry blanket shelters a cloud of earth spouted up, and a small batch of men cleared off from the vicinity of the explosion. It was amusing to see the niggers throw themselves into trenches by the roads and fields. Then came

Oliver Twist on the Veldt.

Pember, of the Sussex, asking for an extra allowance of tea, at the cook-house, while the camp is being shelled by the Boers, at Hekpoort.
(Persuasively) "It may be your last chance, Cookie!"

another and yet another shell, without any more effect than making a hole in a tent, and the men of No. 8 Battery Field Artillery (and No. 8 is a deuced smart Battery, by'r leave) dashed out from their lines, pushing and dragging their guns, while the "4.7 gentleman" began moving his long beak in the air as though sniffing for the foe. "Give 'em hell, boys!" we cried to the busy gunners, as they dashed by us, working at the wheels and drag-ropes, but the Naval man spoke first, "Snap—Bang!" and back the gun jumped in a cloud of smoke; and presently, far away, from the crest of the kopje under suspicion, a cloud of brown arose, and later came the crack of the explosion. Meanwhile the Boers went on pitching shells into our camp, and we got the order to retire behind a kopje with our horses till it was decided what to do with us. Having done this, the shelling soon ceased, and later we were taken back to camp, where we off-saddled, picketed our horses, and settled down to tea. And then *bang! whish! crack!!* bang! whish! towards us the enemy's shells came again. They had got two guns in position, and were working them hard. We were getting some of our own back, for the shells we picked up were 15-pounder ones, of British make. Our Naval gun barked backed viciously at them, and so did the field guns, but the enemy were firing with the red and dazzling setting sun, behind them, and shining directly in our fellows' eyes, who were blazing apparently at poor old Sol, and cussing him and the wily Boer in a manner by no means ambiguous. I know not whether we did them any harm or not; certainly they shifted their positions once or twice. As regards ourselves, it seems beyond belief, no damage was done. The enemy could not even boast of the bag which the Americans achieved at Santiago—that famous mule.

Cattle Lifting. HEKPOORT.

Saturday, September 8th, 1900.

I fancy I stopped in my last near the end of a rather long-winded account of the shelling we experienced at the hands of Brother Boer, on Thursday evening last. To conclude that day's events, we finally shifted our horse lines a bit and turned in, spending a night undisturbed by the distant booming of the Boer guns or the ear-splitting cracking of our 4.7. The next day we returned to our old lines, and settled down for a good day's rest, as we heard that Clements was waiting for Ridley to come up.

I had hardly unsaddled, however, when the sergeant-major came round and told half-a-dozen of us to saddle up and go out with the two guides (civilians, British farmers, who are with this column and know the locality). So we flung on our saddles, and slipping on our bandoliers, mounted and set out in our shirt sleeves (mark that!) with our guides in their civilian togs (mark that!). From these individuals we gathered we were off cattle-lifting, the Boers having left some in a kloof about a couple of miles south of the camp. With jocular allusions to our last quest of a similar nature (the laager near Rustenburg) we smoked and trotted along, comfortable in our shirt sleeves after so much of the usual marching order. Following, came four "boys" to drive the cattle home. We soon reached our objective. The "boys" were sent into the kloof, while we dismounted a little way up the stone-covered kopje on the right, and leaving a couple to look after the gees, the guides and the remainder of us started to climb the heights and cover the "boys" if necessary. Soon a rifle report was heard, and then another. The guides said it was a picket of ours firing on us in mistake from the kopje on the left, and suggested that one of us should work round and let them know who we were. Most of us argued that the report was a Mauser one. However, the guides prevailed, and I was deputed for the job, when the "boys" came running in breathless and told us pantingly that Boers had been sniping them. So seeing that it would be impossible under the circumstances to lift the cattle, we retired on our horses, mounted and moved off. And then the beggars, who had evidently moved up closer, gave it to us fairly warm, and we had to open out and break into a gallop in the direction of the camp. We were about clear of the Mausers and riding through some bush, when, suddenly above a stone wall not a hundred yards in front of us, helmets and heads appeared, also glistening rifle barrels, which pointed, oh no, not on the kopje behind, but on us. [This is where the civilian clothes and shirt sleeves came in.] An officer shouted "Don't fire! Don't fire!!!" Down with those rifles." This order was obeyed reluctantly, then "Who are you?" "Friends! Yeomanry!" "What Yeomanry?" "Sussex." "All right." They proved to be a picket of the Northumberland Fusiliers. Then we crossed a drift, our horses nearly having to swim, and finally reached camp. This morning (Saturday, September 8th) our squadron and the Fifes had to go back about half-a-dozen miles to meet Ridley. Our troop acted as advance party. It was rather an interesting sight to see the two parties meet; the advance of Ridley's force was Kitchener's Horse. When we met, we halted and chatted, waiting for orders. As we did so,

Hate.

the merry snipers started a desultory fire, which gradually became more rapid. Several suspected houses in the vicinity, whose owners had, as usual, taken the oath of neutrality and broken it—*Punica Fides* will have to give way to a new phrase, Boer Faith—were then burnt down. War is not altogether a game, it has its stern aspect. The women and children were loud in their lamentations as the red flames blazed and the dense smoke rolled away on the fresh breeze which was blowing. They cursed us and wept idle tears, but they had their own dear friends, husbands and sons, to thank after all, as nearly all the sniping in this lovely valley is being done by the farmers who live in it. We brought about 25 Boers in camp with us, either suspected or to save them from temptation. To see them, with their roll of blankets, saying good-bye to their weeping families would have touched anything but the hardened, homesick heart of a "Gentleman in Khaki," for he knows full well that the simple peasant in this, as in other localities, usually combines business with pleasure by sniping you in the morning and selling you eggs in the afternoon, as our troop leader puts it.

Sunday, September 9th. A late *reveillé* (6 o'clock). A lovely, lazy day in camp, during which I have been stewing fruit, smoking, and, alas, my bad habits still cling to me, perpetrated for my own amusement a little rough-and-ready rhyme, which I have the temerity to enclose. We had a short service, at which our O.C. Major Percy Browne, a real good man, presided. Ridley, who works with Clements, the same as Mahon did with Ian Hamilton, has with him Roberts' Horse, Kitchener's Horse, some Australians, the 2nd and 6th M.I., some artillery and two pom-poms. We advance to-morrow.

ANOTHER VERSION.

Into our camp, from far away,
Somebody's darling came one day—
Somebody's darling, full of grace,
Wearing yet on his youthful face,
Soon to be hid by a stubbly growth,
The fatted look of a life of sloth.
Thus to our camp, from far away,
Somebody's darling came one day.

Parted and oiled were the locks of gold,
Kissing the brow of patrician mould,
And pale as the Himalayan snows;
Spotlessly clean were his khaki clothes.
It was a cert', beyond any doubt,
Somebody's darling had just come out.

Wond'rous changes were quickly wrought,
Somebody's darling marched and fought.
Somebody's darling learned to shoot,
Somebody's darling loved to loot;
Somebody's darling learned to swear,
And neglected to part his hair.

After riding and marching weary leagues,
Somebody's darling was set on fatigues—
Set on fatigues for dreary hours,
Thinking of home, its fruits and flowers.
Somebody's darling's ideals were quashed;
Somebody's darling went unwashed.

Somebody's darling cussed sergeants big,
Somebody's darling killed a young pig:
Then dressed and trimmed it ready to eat,
First of many a butcherly feat;
Somebody's dear caring naught for looks,
Joined the army of amateur cooks.

Somebody's darling drank water muddy;
Somebody's darling saw men all bloody;
Somebody's darling heard bullets fly;
Somebody's darling saw comrades die;
Somebody's darling was playing the game,—
Thousands and thousands were doing the same.

Somebody's darling rose long before morn;
Somebody's darling went tattered and torn;
Somebody's darling longed for a bite,
Half-baked by day and frozen by night.
Somebody's darling received Mails sometimes,
And his joy was beyond my idle rhymes.

Somebody's darling was sniped one fierce day,
An ambulance jolted him far away;
Somebody's darling had got it bad,
Somebody at home would soon be sad.
Somebody's darling grew worse—then died.
And—that was the end of Somebody's Pride.

Delarey gives us a Field Day.

Monday, September 10th, 1900.

We had *reveillé* at 3.30, and moved off as advance party before dawn. It was not long before we got into action. In less than a mile from our camp we found *frère* Boer, who made his presence known to us in the usual way, that is, with his Mauser, Express, Martini-Henry, or elephant gun; of course, the first is his usual weapon. Not to be too long-winded, we carried ridge after ridge of kopje for several miles. On one occasion the enemy and ourselves rushed for the top of two different kopjes, wherefrom to pepper one another. We only just had time to take cover in a sangar as they opened fire from the opposite hill. Their bullets buzzed and whistled over us, bringing down twigs from a tree just by me, and striking the stones with a nasty sound. Later, the infantry (Worcesters), advancing from behind, began firing over us at the enemy; indeed, for a little time, we were very uncertain whether they were not mistaking us for t'others. Anyhow, their bullets came most infernally close, and necessitated our taking careful cover from the missiles in rear as well as those in front. At last we came to the enemy's main position, which was a fine natural one, and our artillery came into play—we resting for a bit, and the infantry forming up to advance under their fire. Then hell got loose. Bang, bang, bang went our field guns; boom went the 4.7; pom-pom-pom-pom-pom went the Vickers-Maxims; rap-rap-rap-rap-rap-rap went the Maxims; bang, bang went their field guns; up-um, up-um, up-um went their Mausers; crack, crack went our rifles. Imagine the above weapons and a few others, please, all firing, not so much to make themselves heard at the same time (they did that), but to destroy, kill and maim, and you can guess it was hard for a poor tired beggar to sleep. I was fagged out, and when we rested while our gunner friends had their innings, laid down in the blazing noon-day sun, and, with a stone for a pillow, half-dozed for an hour or so. I was roused by a comrade to look in front of me, it was a wonderful sight. About a mile-and-a-half of the Boer position was a blackened line fringed with flame and smoke, but they were still determinedly trying to stop our infantry from occupying a long kopje in front of them, and answering our guns with theirs. That night was almost a sleepless one, for though dead fagged, we all had to do pickets on the ground we had won. The next morning Delarey had disappeared, but we know we shall meet him again.

It is a fine sight to see British infantry advance. With rolled blanket, and mess-tin atop, filled haversack, the accursed "hundred-and-fifty"[*] pulling at his stomach, pipe in mouth, and rifle sloped (butt up as a rule), Mr. Thomas Atkins of the Line goes leisurely forward. I do not know yet what the casualties were. Of the Worcesters who passed

---

[*] The hundred-and-fifty rounds of ammunition which always have to be carried by Thomas Atkins.

us, one poor fellow was shot through the head, and about ten wounded; we had none, save a nag shot by Roberts' Horse in mistake.

Burnt to Death.

HEKPOORT.

Thursday, Sept. 13th, 1900.

We returned to this, our old camp, yesterday, and are resting here for a day or more, one never knows for certain how long these rests will last when out on the war path. Yesterday (the 12th) we had a fairly late *reveillé*, and then, acting as advance guard, returned hither by way of a valley running parallel with this, and through which Ridley advanced when we had our little scrap with Delarey at Boschfontein, on Monday last. By-the-bye, I was yarning, while washing at a stream near here this morning, with some Worcesters, who told me they had five killed and fifteen wounded on that day. Two poor fellows were found burned out of all recognition on the charred veldt the next day. They had been left wounded and had been unable to crawl away from the blazing grass. The valley we passed through yesterday was, in parts, more charming than this. One little village, called Zeekooe, was a particularly pleasant spot, the houses being half-hidden by the white pear blossoms, the pink peach, and the various green foliages of the trees, for this is Spring, when "the young man's fancy lightly turns to thoughts of love," and here am I———, well, well!! Even my old foe, the two-inch thorn bush, has assumed a light-green muslin bridal veil. All this bursting into leaf is most refreshing, to me at least, and I doubt not no less welcome to the noble Boer sniper, who now gets more cover than was possible a month ago. As we left camp, he was sniping away merrily, and about as ineffectively as usual. When we crossed the kopjes to get to this valley we came by way of a fine mountain road. Sheer down below us rushed the river Magaliz, crystal clear, splashing and bubbling over the big rocks in its bed, with weeping willows dipping down from amidst the thick undergrowth on its banks, while now and again a garden from a farm near ran to its edge, with vivid patches of young oats and lemon trees. On arrival in camp, we heard that some Boers had been discovered in some undergrowth, by a stream on our left flank, so we set off, and beating it got six armed.

The barbed-wire curse is great in this Eden-like valley, and when you consider that the advance mounted parties have to go straight ahead through fields and back gardens, the garden walls of which are invariably represented by barbed-wire fencing, you can comprehend that our work is more often than not, no easy matter, especially as wire-nippers are as rare as brandies and sodas, and even when possessed are not much assistance in surmounting the wide and deep irrigation cutting, which is often on the other side of the fence. Again, bogs are not infrequently come across—*across*, by the way, is hardly the word to use. Only a few days ago I was riding towards what I deemed to be a passable ford, when I met a Rough Rider (72nd I.Y.) coming back from it. I casually asked him if it was all right, to which he replied that it was a bit boggy, and then incidentally added, "We've just shot one of our fellows' horses that got stuck and we couldn't get out." Whereupon I took a more circuitous route, a proceeding which I did not regret, when later, I saw the poor, horseless Rough toiling in the broiling sun, his huge saddle covering his head and shoulders, after the tail of the convoy, in hopes of catching it and depositing his burden on a waggon.

The Infection of Spring again.

I must apologise for the enclosed doggerel. Last night, round one of our fires, we were alluding to the various uses we have made of that deadly weapon, the bayonet, and it was suggested that I, as a Spring Poet, should record them in verse, hence the enclosed :—

THE BALLAD OF THE BAYONET.
(Sussex Yeoman *loq.*)
Did I ever use the bay'nit, sir?
In the far off Transvaal War,
Where I fought for Queen and country, sir,
Against the wily Boer.
Aye, many a time and oft, sir,
I've bared the trusty blade,
And blessed the dear old Homeland, sir,
Where it was carefully made.

A YEOMAN'S LETTERS.

Chorus:

Then here's to the British bay'nit
Made of Sheffield steel,
And here's to the men who bore it—
Stalwart men and leal.

You notice the dents on the edge, sir,
At Bronkhurst Spruit they were done;
I was getting a door for a fire,
For out of wood we had run.
I was smiting hard at the door, sir,
Or rafter, I'm not sure which,
When I struck on an iron screw, sir,
And the bay'nit got this niche.

'Tis my mighty Excalibur, sir,
I've used it in joy and grief,
For digging up many a tater,
Or opening bully beef.
I have used it for breaking wire,
Making tents 'gainst rain and sun;
I have used it as a hoof-pick,
In a hundred ways and one.

Oh, how did the point get blunted, sir?
I was driving it home
As a picketing peg for my horse,
So that he should not roam.
I drove it in a little, sir,
And then in my haste, alas,
I stubbed the point on a rock, sir,
Some inches below the grass.

You ask if it e'er took a life, sir?
Aye, I mind the time full well;
I had spotted him by a farm, sir,
And went for him with a yell.
He tried to escape me hard, sir,
But I plunged it in his side,
And there by his own backyard, sir,
A healthy porker died.

But did I draw it in action?
You ask me roughly now.
Yes, we were taking a kopje,
The foe were on the brow.
We drew and fixed our bay'nits,
The sun shone on the steel;
Death to the sniping beggars
We were about to deal.

Then, sweating and a-puffing,
We scaled the rocky height,
But when we reached the top, sir.
The foe was out of sight.

Has it e'er drawn human blood?
Yes, once, I grieve to say;
It was not in a battle,
Or any bloody fray;
'Twas just outside Pretoria.
The deed was never meant,
I slipped and fell on the point, sir,
'Twas quite by accident.

Chorus:
Then here's to the British bay'nit,
Made of Sheffield steel,
And here's to the men who bore it,
Stalwart men and leal.
And here's to the Millenium,
The time of peaceful peace,
When neighbours shall love each other,
And wicked wars shall cease.

Death of Lieutenant Stanley.

Monday, September 17th. There is a funeral to-day—an officer's—and we (the Composite Squadron) are stopping in camp for it, as it concerns us. So I will tell you all about it. Yesterday was Sunday, seldom a day of rest out here. We, the three squadrons of Yeomanry attached to Clements' force, were sent out early on a reconnaissance. Without any opposition we advanced in a westerly direction towards Boschfontein, almost the same way as on Monday last, for about four miles, the Devon and Dorset troops of our squadron being on the right, our Sussex troop on the left, the Rough-riders (72nd I.Y.) in reserve, and the Fife Light Horse scouting ahead. The Fifes had reached the foot of a high grass-covered kopje, and were about to ascend it, when the enemy opened a hot fire on them, causing them to scoot for their lives, which they managed to do successfully. We then galloped up, dismounted, and opened fire on the hill-top, the Devons and Dorsets doing the same on our right, and the Fifes falling back on our left. Where the Roughs were we never knew, probably their officers did. Taking into account the absence of the Nos. 3, with the led horses, and one group of our troop being sent some distance to the left, we only numbered six and our officer, Mr. Stanley, well-known in the cricket world as a Somerset county man. Our led horses were in a donga in the rear. The position we occupied, I should mention, was at the base of a kopje opposite to that held by the Boers. We were sighting at 2,000, when our captain, Sir Elliot Lees, rode up and said he could not make out where the Devons and Dorsets who should have been on our right, were. As a matter of fact they had retired unknown to us. This the wily Boers had seen and quickly taken advantage of, for Sergeant-Major Cave, of the Dorsets, rushing up to us crouching down, told us to fire to our right front, where some trees were about three or four hundred yards away, and from which a heavy fire was being directed at us. Sir Elliot Lees then came up again from our left. Mr. Stanley, seeing the hot corner we were in, retired us about a dozen yards back to the deepest part of the donga, where our led horses were, and ordered the fellows with the horses to retire, and later, gave the command for us to do the same in rushes by threes. Meanwhile our bandoliers were nearly empty, and the Boers were creeping round to our right, which would enable them to enfilade our position. The first three retired, and we were blazing away to cover them, with our heads just showing as we fired over the top of the donga, when the man on my right said, "Mr. Stanley is hit," and looking at him, for he was close to me on my left, I saw he was shot through the head, the blood pouring down his face. Sir Elliot, the other man, and myself were the only ones left in the donga then, so the captain, taking hold of poor Stanley by his shoulders, and I his legs, we started to carry him off. As we picked him up, he insisted, in a voice like that of a drunken man, on somebody bringing his carbine and hat. "Where's my rifle an' hat? Rifle an' hat!" The third man took them and gat—I heard this later. You have no idea what a weight a mortally-wounded man is, and the poor fellow was in reality rather lightly built. On we went, stumbling over stones, a ditch, and into little chasms in the earth. Once or twice he mumbled, "Not so fast, not so fast!" The bullets buzzed, whistled, and hummed by us, missing us by yards, feet, and inches, knocking up the dust and hitting the stones and thorn bushes we staggered through. We, of course, presented a big mark for the Boers, and were not under any covering fire so far as I am aware. The captain, who is grit all through, soon found it impossible to carry the poor fellow by the shoulders, the weight being too much for him, so I offered, and we changed places, Sir Elliot taking his legs and on we went, pausing, exhausted, perspiring and breathless, now and again, for a rest. At last, turning to our left, we reached a little bit of cover, thanks to a friendly rise in the ground, and falling into a kind of deep rut with Stanley's body on top of me, I waited while the captain went to see if he could get any assistance. Presently he returned with a Somerset man; and a minute or so later a Fife fellow, a medical student, came up. The former and I then got him on a little farther. After a few minutes' deliberation, the captain said, reluctantly, "we must leave him." We all three asked permission to stay. To which Sir Elliot replied, "I don't want to lose an officer and three men. Come away, men!" We then moved the poor fellow into a cutting about two feet deep and three feet wide, and arranged a haversack under his head. As we loitered, each unwilling to leave him first, Sir Elliot thundered at us to come on, saying, "I don't know why it is, but a Yeoman never will obey an order till you've sworn at him." Then reluctantly we set off in single file, working our way back by the bank of a stream, and still under cover of the rise in the ground, a little way up which we found one of our Sussex men, with his horse bogged to the neck. Further on we paused a moment, and the Fife man, saying that he thought the wound was not mortal, suggested that it would be well for somebody to be with Stanley so as to prevent him from rolling on it, and then asked permission to return. My Fife friend had not seen what I had. He had only seen where the bullet went in, not where it came out. Seeing that the captain was about to give him permission, I said "Mr. Stanley is my officer, sir, and I have the right to go," and he let me. I gave one my almost-empty bandolier, and another my haversack, telling him it contained three letters for the post, and—if necessary, to post them. My rifle I had already thrown into a ditch at Sir Elliot's command. Then I worked my way back, hoping that I should not be shot before reaching him. I got there all right, and evidently unseen; lying down by him, I arranged my hat so as to keep the sun off his face, and cutting off part of my left shirt-sleeve, with the water from my bottle, used half of it to bathe his temples and wipe his bubbling, half-open mouth. The other I moistened, and laid over the wound. He was quite unconscious, of course, and his case hopeless. Once I thought he was gone, but was mistaken. The second time, however, there was no mistake.

I waited by the brave man—who had been our troop leader for the last fortnight, and who had, I am sure, never known fear—for some time deliberating what to do. Shots were still being fired from somewhere in my vicinity, while our firing I had gloomily noted had receded, and finally ceased. By-and-bye, all was silent, then a bird came and chirped near me and a butterfly flitted by. At length, as it appeared to me useless to wait by a dead man, I determined to get back to camp, if possible, instead of waiting to be either shot in cold blood, or made a prisoner. After carefully going through all his pockets, from which I took his purse, watch, whistle, pipe, pouch, and notebook, and, attaching his glasses to my belt, having arranged him a little and laid my bloody handkerchief over his face, I got up, and worked my way along by the river bank till compelled to go into the open. I trusted to a great extent to my khaki on the dry grass, and daresay it saved me from making much of a mark; but spotted I was, and from the right and left the bullets came very thick and unpleasantly close. For about a mile I was hunted on the right and left like a rabbit. At first I ran a little, but was done, and soon dropped into a staggering walk. After a while I came on Dr. Welford and his orderly behind some rocks, just coming out, but when he heard my news he turned back, and, as I refused to use his horse, which he offered me, at my request rode off, and got potted at a good deal. Further on, he waited for me. He is a brick, our doctor; and when he learnt I was thirsty, and he saw my tired condition (the sun on my bare head had been most unpleasant) he offered me a drop of whisky and water, adding, "You'd better have it when we get round the bend of the kopje ahead." I thanked him, and said I thought it would be more enjoyable *there*. Enjoy it I did. Finally I reached the camp and told the captain the sad news, at the same time handing in the gallant officer's belongings. His watch was at 12.5 when I left him. Sir Elliot was most kind to me, and said I had acted gallantly, and he had told the major (commanding us). Then Major Browne came up, and he was also very complimentary. Of course, there was nothing in what I had done that any other man would not have done, and I told them so, especially as the example set by the captain made it impossible for a man to be other than cool. Lieutenant Stanley, who took command of us when we left Pretoria a fortnight ago, had soon become very popular, for he was a thorough sportsman, keen as mustard, quite unaffected and absolutely fearless. I feel pleased with myself for taking everything off the poor fellow before I left him; for when, late last night, the ambulance came in with him, the doctor's orderly told me that they found him stripped of his boots, gaiters, and spurs —which was all that were left worth taking.

His Burial.

> "And far and wide,
>   They have done and died,
>   By donga, and veldt, and kloof,
>   And the lonely grave
>   Of the honored brave,
>   Is a proof—if we need a proof."
>   *E. Wallace.*

Tuesday, September 18th. We buried Lieut. Stanley yesterday at mid-day, the sergeants acting as bearers, we Sussex men (of the dozen of us, two were with him at Eton and one at Oxford) composed the firing party, while the whole squadron, officers and men followed. About three-quarters of a mile from our present camp, in the garden of a Scotchman, named Jennings, by a murmuring, running stream, and beneath some willows, we laid him. By the side of the grave was a bush of Transvaal may, covered in white blossom, at the end were roses to come, and away back and front were the white-covered pear trees and pink-covered peach, perfuming the clear, fresh air, while on the sides of the babbling stream were ferns and a species of white iris. Sewn up in his rough, brown, military blanket, he was lowered to his last resting-place, the major reading the Burial Service.

"—— Is cut down like a flower."

He could not have been more than twenty-five. Then, "Fire three volleys of blank ammunition in the air. Ready! Present! Fire!" Again and again, and the obsequies of a brave officer and true English gentleman and sportsman were over.

I am sorry to say that we have a Sussex sergeant missing—killed or prisoner. We are most anxious to know his fate, poor fellow. So, out of the seven of us in that hot corner, one is dead, one is not, and Heaven only knows how the others escaped, myself in particular.

Wednesday, September 19th. This morning we advanced about half-a-dozen miles, and pitched our camp here—Doornkloof is the name of the place, I believe.

Thursday, September 20th. Ridley's column has gone back in the direction of Pretoria to Rietfontein, as escort to a convoy, principally composed of waggons loaded with oat hay. I hear, and hope it is true, that he has our letters.

Friday, September 21st. Had to do a picket on an outlying kopje. The stable guard, who should have *reveilléd* us at three forgot to do so, and later, when we were aroused, we had to saddle up and clear off at once. I had to go off *sans café* (which is breakfast), and worse still in my hurry *sans* pipe. Oh, how that worried me, my pipe which I have kept and smoked through all till now. Somebody might tread on it and break it, or find it and not return it. On the kopje a friend lent me his emergency pipe, over which a lot of quinine powder had been upset, so I had a few smokes, in which the flavour of quinine prevailed unpleasantly. Still, I have no doubt it was healthy. But, oh, where was my pipe, should I ever see it again? "There is a Boer outpost over there." "Yes, but I wonder what the deuce has become of my pipe," and then I bored my vigilant fellow sentinel with the history of that pipe. With the sun pouring down on us without shelter, without any grub, and not a drop of water (my bottle I left by Stanley), we were stuck up on that kopje till past sunset. Where was my pipe, should I get it all right? At last we got back to camp, and, overjoyed, I received from a friend my pipe, which he had picked up in the lines. Then, having partaken of tea, I found myself in for a sleepless night as stable picket. But it didn't matter, I had got my pipe.

Saturday, September 22nd.

> "There is a foe who deals hard knocks,
> In a combat scarce Homeric:
> It's *not* the Boer, who snipes from rocks,
> But fever known as Enteric."

The idea I have partly expressed in the above lines, is as you know, correct. The Boer from behind his rock snipes you at a distance, but Sister Enteric, though unseen, as Brother Boer, is nearer to us. She is with us in our camps, when we eat and when we drink—often parched, recklessly drink—and close, unseen and unheard, deals her blows. And when they are dealt, the nervous ones amongst us *think*. For common report hath it that the illness takes roughly about three weeks to develop, and the nervous man thinks back what did he drink three weeks ago, or thinking of what he ate or drank the day before, dreads the developments three weeks may bring. When we came in last night we heard that a poor fellow of our squadron had succumbed to it, and was to be buried the next morning at 5.30. We bury soon out here. So once again this week, I formed a unit of the firing party, and did the slow march with reversed arms. We clicked the three volleys at the grave. Later, we had two more funerals, the result of Brother Boer's handiwork. They were two men of Kitchener's Horse, who had dropped behind Ridley's force at Hekpoort, and had ridden to Mrs. Jennings' farm to buy some bread. These two were shot by over half-a-dozen concealed Boers at about twenty yards range. No attempt was made to make them prisoners, and they were practically unarmed, having revolvers only. Their bodies were riddled.

Sunday, September 23rd.

> "Oh, happy man in study quiet,
> On data and statistics,
> Making copy of our diet,
> Please soften our biscuits!"

This afternoon having borrowed a magazine from a Rough, in exchange for an old one I picked up in the Fife lines, I have in common with the sharer of my blanket shelter derived infinite entertainment from an article therein contained, entitled "Feeding the Fighting Man." Of course, it is illustrated with photographs, the first one depicting a sleek and stiff Yeomanic-looking, khaki-clad being standing by the side of a swagger little drawing-table covered with a fringed tablecloth, and obviously groaning under what we learn are the gentleman's daily rations. Apart from the article, this picture alone is calculated to make one's mouth water. The article opens with an extract from that great book, "The Soldier's Pocket Book." Here it is, "It may be taken as an accepted fact that the better the men are fed the more you will get out of them, the better will be their health and strength, the more contented will they be, and the better will be their discipline," all of which is gospel truth. The article, as I have already remarked, is very entertaining. Here is a little extract—"fresh meat and bread have been issued daily, almost without a single exception, to troops at the front." We know the fresh meat, good old trek ox ! Always delightfully fresh—and tough, And the bread, yes, the bread, well-er-the bread, yes, the bread! If I had read this article at home, being somewhat of a gourmand, I should certainly have rushed off and enlisted directly after reading as far as the middle, where we learn that every soldier is allowed daily—oh, the list is too long to give you. There is one little thing the scribe overlooked, and that is the waggon crowd, the quartermaster-sergeant and his satellites. It may also be of interest to you to know that certain non-coms. and men of the A.S.C. have made large sums of money out here. I have heard of one who made three or four hundred pounds in a few months, hem ! Of course, they are exceptions in a corps which has, as everyone knows, done grand work. Our running commentaries as I read the article through, would have made excellent marginal reading, if such notes could have been added for a future edition.

Yesterday, a fresh epidemic visited our camp—football. Some person, evilly disposed I presume, produced a football which after a "good blow out" (oh, happy football) was kicked in the midst of a crowd of wild enthusiasts. We soon had a casualty, a sergeant stubbing his big toe badly on a boulder; now he can hardly walk. I believe there were a few other minor casualties. Thirty enteric cases were taken into Pretoria with the last convoy. I am slowly but surely learning to spread jam very thinly on biscuit, one of the most difficult accomplishments I have had to learn out here. My jam spreading having hitherto been at once the scandal and horror of my messmates.

On Monday morning one of Bethune's Horse came into our camp, he had been a Boer prisoner, and had escaped from Rustenburg, which they are at present occupying (I think it is their turn this month). He had been wandering for fourteen days, or rather nights, for it was then he travelled—a native chief had supplied him with a guide, who piloted him about, and kept him going on berries and such like. He said to me, "I was glad to see English faces again," and I, who in a small way know what it is to be hunted, believed him, you bet.

Promoted to Full Corporal.

Tuesday, September 25th. Yesterday we moved out to meet and escort Ridley in with the convoy from Pretoria. About a couple of miles out we heard guns, and I thought probably we should have a bit of scrapping, but we did not beyond some half-hearted sniping. To my surprise and delight Ridley brought mails, my portion being eleven letters. Some had the home post mark of May 25th, and the others August 7th. I must leave off for a space here, as I have to carve an epitaph for the poor fellow who died a few days ago. You see one's occupations out here are many and varied.

(Resumed.)

Yesterday evening the orderly sergeant came down to my wigwam, and asked for my regimental number, which I gave him without asking the reason why. Soon he returned and congratulated me, saying I had been promoted to full corporal over poor Stanley's affair. My many comrades also have warmly congratulated me on my return to my former state, or rather above it, for it is a case of wearing two stripes now.

Wednesday, September 26th. On this day we advanced. Our column did not come in for the usual amount of attention from our friend the enemy, the reason being that a gentleman friend of ours, General Broadwood, was pounding away at them from one side, and Ridley from another. All the same we had a very busy day, scouting and occupying kopjes. Our guns fired at some Boer waggons, causing their escort to clear, and leave them for us. Our infantry got them and had a good time. They are fine fellows, are our infantry, and deserve all they can get in the loot line. Late in the afternoon we surrounded a suspicious-looking kloof, full of thick undergrowth, and captured a couple of the peaceful peasants of the Arcadian dorp (fontein, kloof or spruit) we were then occupying. A man in quest of loot found them, to his great surprise. They were of the *genus snipa*. One had an elephant gun and the other a Martini. We had had *reveillé* at 2.30, and breakfast a little later. From then till about six in the evening I had only a few bits of biscuit, and once a drop of water, but felt none the worse for my little fast.

Thursday, September 27th. We got us up at 3.30. On going to saddle up I found that my horse was gone. However, after a careful search, I found him, though he had changed colour and size. When in the Yeomanry, do as the Yeomen do. So having got a mount I was soon on parade. We then ascended a big kopje and were placed at various observation posts till such time as the convoy should move off. On the top of this kopje were numerous tree-locusts. these are far more swagger in appearance than their khaki-clad brethren, being green and yellow, with a crimson and purple lining to their wings; but their whole appearance is so artificial, that my first impression on seeing one was that it had flown out of a Liberty Shop. From the various uncomplimentary remarks one hears passed on the locust, I imagine the name must be derived from the expression "low cuss." At 3.30 the tail of the beastly but necessary convoy had succeeded in negotiating the usual non-progressive drift, and we left our kopje to form its rear guard. My horse and I went a lovely howler soon after starting—my first spill. I got up feeling all the better for the experience, and soon had another. In this my rifle got broken.

Friday, September 28th. We arrived at Olifant's Nek with the convoy at 3.30 a.m. a bit tired, found lukewarmed-up tea, bully and biscuits awaiting us, and then turned in, and just and unjust slumbered soundly till a late *reveillé*, 6 o'clock, bundled us out to feed our horses. My latest acquisition I found had vamoosed or been vamoosed. In searching for it, I found my old one. Then, having foraged around at our waggon and secured a Lee-Metford, I was once again fully equipped. At about 10, we advanced through the bush veldt as far as our present camping ground, which is called Doornlaagte, I believe.

Saturday, September 29th. As we are resting here to-day I will continue my diary-like letter.

(Resumed.)

My fell intentions of writing this morning were knocked on the head, as we had to go out on a patrol. Our latest *rôles* being that of resurrectionists, or grave desecrators. The reason was that certain tombs had been regarded with grave suspicion (I beg your pardon) our "intelligence" people imagining them to contain buried arms, ammunition, or treasure. However, on our arrival at the spot, a close inspection made it evident that they were *bonâ-fide* affairs, not Mauser-leums, and by no means new as reported, so we left the rude forefathers of the hamlet undisturbed.

Sunday, September 30th. We have just marched back from Doornlaagte through Olifant's Nek, and are camped here, a mile beyond. To-day is a regular Sunday-at-Home day. It has been quite a record day, especially for a Sabbath, for we have not heard a single Mauser go off.

Monday, October 1st. Another month! Actually a year ago this month the war commenced, and there are still corners on the slate unwiped, and we, the poor wipers, are industriously wiping, and certainly cannot complain of a lack of rags. We moved out from the Nek through Krondaal and camped at Sterkstrom. Amongst the latest reports, false and true, we heard in the evening that the C.I.V.'s were off —homeward bound.

Tuesday, October 2nd. The previous night we heard that the camp would not be shifted, nor was it. But we, of the Yeomanry, were. At 3.30, therefore, we had to arise and go out with the guns to co-operate with Ridley and Broadwood. After manœuvring about, we were finally posted on what at first appeared a kopje of no importance (in height and composition), but kopjes were deceivers ever, and when we had got half-way up, those that had sufficient breath and energy left to express their opinions on kopjes in general, and this one in particular, did so. However, once up aloft, we were left undisturbed for the remainder of the day. On return to camp we found our missing sergeant (of September 16th, at Hekpoort). He had been a prisoner in Rustenburg and had got his liberty when Broadwood occupied or rather re-occupied the town. Whenever we go out one way the Boers come in the other, and *vice versa*. Though we had not played an active part in the day's operations, the others had, and the outing was rather a success, Ridley's men capturing fourteen waggons with ammunition and other stuff and a few prisoners.

Thursday, October 4th. Once again our fond hopes of a day's loaf were crushed, for it was "up in the morning early," and hie for Bethanie. This little native town we reached and surrounded, and then destroyed a mill. On the way there we came on a recently-deserted waggon (a pot of coffee was boiling over a small fire). This and its contents we destroyed; and back, which was by a different road, we came upon and destroyed four or five waggons by burning them.

* * * * *

The effect of Army, or rather Yeomanry life, its fatigues and worries, big and small, on men hitherto unaccustomed to such things, has been marvellous, and productive of a topsy-turvy dom of character, after Mr. W. S. Gilbert's own heart. To commence with, it is curious to note that in many cases men who claim to have roughed it in various parts of the world have been amongst the worst to stand the roughing here, and while weak-looking striplings have developed into fine hardy men; brawny, massive-looking fellows have shrunk to thin and useless beings. As regards character, after about four to six months out here one seems to see his fellows in all the nakedness of truth. I have seen the genial man turn irritable, the generous man mean, the good-tempered man quarrelsome, the smart and particular man slovenly, the witty man dull, the bow-and-arrow ideal (looking) *sabreur* anything but dashing in action, the old-womanly man indifferent to danger, and the objectionable man the best of comrades. These and other changes have I noted, and often fearfully thought how have I changed, how has it affected me, but

> "There is no grace the giftie to gie me,
> To see mysel' as ithers see me."

and perhaps it is as well.

Petty Annoyances—The Nigger.

Friday, October 5th. We marched into Commando Nek this morning, and are now camped here (when I use the word "camped," I hope you do not think I mean tents and such-like luxurious paraphernalia, because I don't). Our

"Mails up for the Devons, Dorsets & Fifes! None for the Sussex!!!"

(Please observe the Sussex men on the right)

lines have by no means fallen in a pleasant place, being on dusty ground by the side of the road which goes through the Nek, along which for the last two hours about half-a dozen miles of convoy has been proceeding *en route* for Rustenburg, and what with the yelling of the black man and (a hundred-times-removed) brother—I allude to the blooming niggers—the lowing of the oxen, and the dust—well, " it ain't all lavender," neither is it conducive to letter-writing or good temper. But to own up, the above would not trouble us a bit, if we had only received our mails, which we have not. I had been looking forward to a fine batch and relying on getting them with a faith which would have removed kopjes, and now I am disappointed. The bitterness of the whole thing is that some one has blundered, for the Fifes in front have theirs, and the Rough Riders behind have theirs, but we, the Composite Squadron, are without ours. *Donnerwetter und Potztausand!* There, I had intended writing and telling you how much I am really enjoying myself, of the beauties of the veldt, its pretty little flowers, the multi-coloured butterflies and insects, the glorious open-air life we are leading and a' that ; and here I am like a bear with a sore head, grumbling, grumbling, grumbling. And now the companion of my shelter and sharer of my mealie pap—I call him *Cœur de Lion* (I don't mind him having the heart of a lion, but I object to him having its appetite)—is growling, and wanting to know "when the Yeomanry are going home. We came out for a crisis, and if the authorities call this a crisis may he be—" etc., etc., as he certainly will. I have tried to pacify him with the following offering of the muse—but failed :—

"Great Bugs of State. Imperial Bugs,
The time grows heavy on our hands;
Are the recruiting sergeants dead?
Does khaki fail, or martial bands?
Oh, teach the vagrant how to ride,
The orphan boy to meet the foe;
May Heaven melt your stony hearts,
To let the foolish Yeoman go."

Being under the impression that I have not made any direct reference to the nigger, of whom, of course, one sees a great deal, I will here give you my condensed opinion of this being. Left in his true state, he is, I believe, unobjectionable, but we have spoilt him. Our fellows have been too familiar with him in camp and on the march, and you know what familiarity breeds. He has sat or stood idle and watched with indifference we white men in khaki doing work he should have been set to do (I have borne huge sacks and other burdens, and cursed the officers, who have not made use of the niggers standing idly by). He has had the satisfaction of knowing that while he is earning three or four shillings a day, Thomas Atkins is earning thirteenpence. The general result is that he has become deucedly independent and occasionally confoundedly cheeky. As a remedy, I would suggest at the conclusion of this war—that is, assuming it does conclude—97 per cent. of the niggers employed by the British Government be jolly well kicked and then set in bondage for half-a-dozen years, more if their case requires it.

Our horses are nearly all done. Mine is very lame in its hind legs. As far as horseflesh goes, he is the least objectionable brute I have had, though his ignorance and lack of appreciation of kindness is appalling. We have drawn horseshoes for five weeks, so it does not look like returning to Pretoria just yet. If we had drawn horses it would have been more to the purpose. We are having tea now, and have just drawn our biscuits for the next 24 hours. They number four thinnish ones, and represent three-quarter rations. Even as regards biscuits, one learns a good deal out here. I myself know four kinds of biscuits, all as like as any of Spratt's gold medal ones in appearance, but varying greatly in taste, and consequently, popularity.

A Wet Night.

COMMANDO NEK,

Sunday, October 7th, 1900.

As you can see by the above, we are still here, but expect to move to-morrow.

Yesterday was hot and windy, but, beyond one incident, uneventful. Late in the day indigo, watery-looking clouds in the west caused some of us to erect blanket shelters for the coming night, and when the evening having come, a flash of lightning and a distant peal of thunder, followed by a few spatters of rain, heralded what was to come, we wise virgins (pardon the simile) huddled in our booby hutches (unfortunately *without* lamps) and congratulated ourselves on our astuteness. Soon it came, the lightning flashing, the thunder crashing, the rain pouring, and lastly the wind blowing a perfect tornado. The various jerry-built domiciles stood it well for some time, then the hutch behind us was blown down, and we in ours roared with glee; then another went, and finally the wind, not being able to get at us by a frontal attack, took us on the flank, and up blew one blanket, and the rifles at the ends wavered. Then, with cries of "Close the water-tight compartments," "Man the pumps," "Launch the lifeboat," "Where's the rocket apparatus?" and such-like remarks, as used by those in peril on the sea, we came out and joined in the fun. The horses, seeing us all about, thought it must be *reveillé*, and started neighing and pawing the ground, expecting their grub. We were soon inside again under jury-rigging, and went off to sleep to the shouts of "Stable guard, here's a horse loose!" "Stable guard, here are three horses walking over us!" and the reply, "All right, I'm coming round in the captain's dinghy," or some such rejoinder. I could not help smiling when one of our fellows, in response to a cry of "Buck up, boys of the bull-dog breed!" remarked, "Hang it, they don't even give us kennels." In the small hours of the morning our hutch collapsed again, and with the blanket on my side supported mainly on my nose, I heedlessly slumbered on. At *reveillé* the greeting we gave one another was "Oh, what a night!" The Roughs were in a particularly happy frame of mind, though they had slept in the open, for their officers' tent had come down, also their sergeants', and the remarks of the former, "Aw, Frisby, have you got that wope?" "Where's that beastly peg?" "Heah, give me the hammah," "Isn't it awful?" had been most soothing to them. Although I did my best to protect my few remaining envelopes, I have just discovered three of them to be well gummed down. One thing must be said to the credit of the rain, *it has laid the dust,* and that is no small matter.

Monday, October 8th. Having had no mails, we sallied forth with Mr. Clements in the direction of Krugersdorp, with four days' rations. My last charger being done, *I've got another 'oss*, and he seems rather a good one, though not up to my weight. Last night it came to my ears that the Border Regiment had got their dry canteen up from Pretoria, and it would be open for an hour or so, and that chocolate, jam, cocoa paste, tobacco and other coveted commodities would be on sale. So I was soon mingling with the crowd of would-be purchasers; several of our fellows also joined the crowd, but when it came to their turn to buy were turned away because they belonged not to the Border Regiment. I, however, had not my hat or tunic on, and as there was nothing about my shirt or general appearance to distinguish me from Mr. Thomas Atkins of the Border Regiment, I succeeded in buying four packets of chocolate and several tins of potted meats and jams; then, handing my purchases over to a friend, I again took up my position at the end of the queue and bought some more stuff. The prices were what is commonly known as popular prices, being extraordinarily low for this benighted land. As our four days' rations simply consist of four of the least popular brand of biscuits imaginable per diem and horrible stewed trek ox, these little purchases are coming in very handy. We camped early in the afternoon on the high veldt. The night was bitterly cold.

The Great Egg Trick.

Wednesday, October 10th.
"When scouting and you must not tarry,
Of things you can borrow or beg,
The best, but the worst you can carry,
Is the excellent, succulent *egg*."
Extract from contemplated "*Loot Lyrics.*"

To-day we have returned to Commando Nek, at least within a mile or so of it. (A cart has just come in from Rietfontien, and they say there are four bags of mails for the Composites, so we poor Sussex de'ils ought to have a look in.) We were advance party to-day, and a friend and I had the good luck to get a fine lot of eggs, of which I have not had any for a long time. As you may imagine, eggs are not very easily carried by the uninitiated, especially when he happens to be a horseman. The first time I managed to get some I got a couple from a farm down the next valley, and was debating how I should carry them, when the officer of our troop, who was just ahead, turned round and sternly told me to mount and get forward, and as he stopped for me to do so, I was rather awkwardly situated, my rifle being in one hand and the two eggs in the other. However, I seized the reins somehow or other, and did the great egg trick successfully. Missing other feats in which I have never once broken or cracked even one, to-day I eclipsed all previous accomplishments, inasmuch as I carried in the only two tunic pockets I have without holes, THREE DOZEN EGGS loose, and despite having to dismount and mount twice, brought them into camp without breaking or cracking one. Once or twice, when we had to do a trot, our sergeant-major asked why I was riding so curiously, and I told him I was feeling rather queer, but thought it would wear off when I reached camp—it did. A friend and I got these eggs in rather an amusing manner. We spotted a Kaffir village and riding to it, enquired at every kraal for eggs, "Eggs for the general—for Lord Roberts!" but, alas, they had none, "I'kona," signifying the negative. One enterprising youth. however, called to me as I was riding off and brought me four, for which I paid him sixpence. Then once again as we were going away, he called to us—evidently the pay, pay, pay of the absent-minded foreign devil has touched his savage heart—for lo and behold his neighbours had some for sale, and came forward with a dozen in a tin, then their neighbours came to the front with about a score, and yet another lot appeared with more—in all, we got fifty eggs, of which I pocketed three dozen, and carried the remainder in a handkerchief and surrendered them to our major, saying I had got them for him (he was in want of some), and thus appeased him. Had I carried them all in my *mouchoir* I might have lost the lot, but we simple Yeomen "know a thing or three," as the ancient ballad goes.

We have just drawn rations for fourteen days and been joined by some more M.I., so it looks as if

"Troops may come and troops may go,
But we go on for ever."

" Go hon ! " seems to be our call and counter cry.

COMMANDO NEK, *Friday, October 12th,* 1900.
Excerpt from proposed Christmas Panto.
Place—The Transvaal. Period—Victorian.
Officers' Tent.

First Officer: "I heah the men are gwousing about their gwub."

Second Officer: "Er—I think they get their wations wegularly."

Third Officer: "Oh, dem! They're alwight. Anyhow, what do they want with gwub? A little more turkey and peas, and—er pass the whisky, Fwed,"

The Waggon.

Quartermaster-Sergeant (to kindred spirit): "Look 'ere; twelve tins of bacon, sixteen of jam, biscuits, and a jar of rum. Lemme see; there's twelve of us, and twenty of them. 'Umph, that's eight tins of bacon and eleven of jam for us, and four of bacon and five of jam for them. Let 'em 'ave four biscuits a man; save the best for us—don't forget—"

Kindred Spirit: "And the rum?"

Quartermaster-Sergeant: "Confound it; I nearly forgot that. Oh—er—er—take 'em a cupful, and—er—say we're on half rations."

Chorus from minor waggonites from round cook-house fire.

"We don't want to fight,
And, by Jingo, if—we—do,
We've got the rum, we've got the tea,
And we've got the sugar, too."

The Yeomen's Lines. Men just in from patrol.

Man with bullet hole in hat: "Is tea up?"

Enter orderly corporal with rations: "I say, you fellows, it's 'damall' again to day."

Chorus: "! ! ! ? ? ? * * *"

Of course it is evident to you that the above extracts are from a burlesque written by a man in the ranks. Alas! there is a perpetual feud existent between "the brave, silent men at the back," and ditto those at the front, consequently any joke at the expense of the "waggon crowd" is always appreciated beyond its value. Sergeant-Major Hunt, who had been acting as quartermaster-sergeant for several weeks, did us remarkably well; but, alas, he has been invalided into Pretoria, and another has reigned in his stead, who has done evil in (or rather out of) our sight; being either incompetent or too clever. By the foregoing, you can see that I have not got much news to record. We expect some of the time-expired Police to join us on Sunday or Monday, and so, I fancy, we shall not move till they come up.

Our Friend "Nobby."

We often get some of the Border men in our lines, and, like all of the Regulars, they are most entertaining, though their statements usually require a few grains of salt

'Nobby.'

before swallowing. One of these bold Border men, known to us as "Nobby," is awfully disgusted at my bad habit of letter writing. As a rule I am scribbling when he strolls up, and get greeted with the jeering remark, "At it again." Some days back, after reflectively expectorating, he delivered himself thus on letter writing: "I don't often write. When I do, I sez 'I'm all right; 'ow's yerself?' A soldier's got too much to do to write blooming letters." Then he retailed terrible stories of Spion Kop, Pieter's Hill, and other affairs. Amongst his loot stories I know the following to be a fact; its hero has since been court-martialled. One of the men in Clements' Force, being *en route*, visited a house, and, producing his emergency rations (these are contained in a curious little tin case), threatened to blow the house and its occupants to kingdom-come unless they complied with his request for eggs, bread, coffee, etc. They complied, but, unfortunately for the man in question, a nigger belonging to the place followed him into camp, and reported the case. Mr. Thomas Atkins of the Line has curious notions about the distances he marches. Of course, he is a grand marcher, and has done remarkable distances and times in this campaign; still, occasionally he makes one smile, when it is a known fact that the Force has just covered ten miles, by emphatically swearing that his battalion has done twenty. For cheeriness, the fellows I have met would take a lot of beating, and their pride in their own particular regiments is a very pleasing trait, though frequently it leads them to be rough on other by no means unworthy corps.

From the dry canteen of the Border Regiment I was fortunate enough yesterday to procure two dozen boxes of matches, a packet of six candles, a quarter-of-a-pound of Navy Cut, notepaper and envelopes. The latter I got none too soon, as my last gumless envelope I stuck down with jam. Candles are a luxury I have been without for many months, and matches have been worth sixpence a box. I bought them at a penny, and the candles at 1/6 the packet. We have the Yorkshire Light Infantry with us now in place of the Worcesters.

Saturday, October 13th.
   The law which sways our generals' ways,
    Is mystery to me;
   Though we of course, both foot and horse
    Fulfil each strange decree.

This morning we had *reveillé* at five and moved off up the

valley at about seven, the Infantry going on the Magaliesberg. This being the case, of course our progress was slow, and the distance covered at the most six miles. We are going to be joined in a few days' time by detachments of our Police, who are coming out from the flesh pots of Pretoria. Two Sussex officers are coming with them and we expect about fifty men. To-day I had to go into a barn and pry about for arms and ammunition on the off chance. I did not find anything in that line, but got covered with fleas, a hundred or so—so I have been well occupied since I have been in camp. We rode through some grand crops of oats, wheat and barley; in one field the wheat was so high as to reach to our horses' ears. Where I got my fleas, or rather they got me, there was a grand garden with orange trees (no fruit), peaches coming on, figs also, and pomegranates in blossom. In a corner of this deserted garden I came across a real, old-fashioned English rose, of the kind usually and irreverently called "cabbage." The occasion seemed to call for an effort, so here it is:

  An old-fashioned English rose
  In the far-off Transvaal land;
  Smelt by an English nose,
  And plucked by an English hand.

This evening we had tents served out to us. Last night we had a deal of thunder and lightning, but no rain. It was very close, and most of us slept, or tried to sleep, in our shirt-sleeves. About four days before, on the high veldt, we had frost on our blankets in the morning.

Monday, October 15th. Yesterday we only marched a few miles, and to-day we have done even less. The Infantry marching along the Magaliesberg searching the kloofs, farms at the base, and such-like, rendering progress, of necessity, slow. Behind us, every day now, we leave burning houses and waggons. Colonel Legge, who has taken over Ridley's command, is doing the same a little ahead of us on our left front, and Broadwood likewise on the other side of the Magaliesberg. Since leaving Commando Nek our column has found and destroyed nearly three dozen good waggons and numerous deserted farms. It seems rather rough, but leniency has proved the stumbling block of the campaign, and now we are doing what any other than a British Army would have done months ago. Our camp is near a deserted farm. The house is, of course, now gutted out, but around it are fields of bearded barley, golden wheat and oats, a lovely grove of limes, and rows of ripening figs, peaches and red blossoming pomegranates. This morning I had a fine bathe in a pool near by, and was washing my one and only shirt, when I heard that honey was being got near the lime grove, so jumped into my breeks and boots, and tying my wet shirt round my neck, rushed up to have a look in. A lot of silly, laughing niggers were the principal *personæ* in the little comedy. There were two or three hives, and after a little smoking I went and helped myself; at the next hive I did pretty well, but at the next, after I had inserted my hand into it and taken several pieces of comb, the bees went for us in style. I had put on my shirt by that time, fortunately for me; as it was, I had them buzzing all round my head, and got fairly well stung; two got into one of my boots and jobbed their tails, which were hot, into my bare ankle, several stung my hands, arms and forehead, and one got me exactly on the tip of my nose. However, I have felt no inconvenience from any of the stings, in spite of being without the blue-bag. Our reinforcements of ex-Police have not turned up yet; we are looking forward to seeing them, because they are sure to bring our mails. My horse has developed a bad off hock, now. Like the poet:

"I never had a decent horse,
Which was a treat to ride,
But came the usual thing, of course,
It sickened or it died."

Tuesday, October 16th. The animal referred to above went a lovely purler with me this morning, turning a somersault and finishing by laying across my right leg. It was some time before I could get help, and then only a man came and sat on the brute's head to keep him down. I was grasping his two hind hoofs, which were within a few inches of my face, and preventing them from "pushing it in." At length, the doctor and his orderly galloped up, and the latter, dismounting, grasped the horse's tail, and pulled him off far enough for me to free my leg. Apart from rather a bad back, I am all serene.

Our friend, "Nobby of the Borders," visited us last night. I don't think that is his real name, and am not anxious to know. To us he is, and always will be, "Nobby." He was tired, having been on the kopjes for the best part of the day, but interesting as ever.

"Art thou weary, art thou langwidge?"

he quoted after a reflective expectoration, which just missed my right foot. "That's a hymn, ain't it?" he queried with the air of a man of knowledge. We replied in the affirmative, and then, curious to hear his religious convictions, asked him about them. "Yes, I believe in religion," said Nobby, "I was confirmed and converted or whatever it is, some time ago. And I tell you, since I've been out 'ere in this war I've felt certain about Gawd. Spion Kop and Pieter's 'Ill made yer think, I can tell yer." And then waxing wrath about certain of his comrades, he inveighed thus: "And yet there's some —— —— fellers in the reg'ment 'oo will —— —— say there ain't a Gawd. But those —— —— —— beggars are always —— —— arguing about every —— thing." If Mr. Burdett-Coutts wants any corroboration in respect to his exposure of the inner working of certain military hospitals, let him apply to Private "Nobby" of the Borderers. He was an enteric patient at No. 1 Field Hospital, Modderspruit, and the tales he tells of his own uncared-for sufferings, and the even worse ones of comrades, show, alas, that the hospital can, and does often contain, as well as kind, self-sacrificing, skilful doctors, doctors and medical orderlies who are brutal, selfish, and absolutely callous. He speaks well of the nurses, I am glad to say.

"The Roughs" leave us for Pretoria.

NOOITGEDACHT,
(A little beyond Hekpoort).

Wednesday, October 17th, 1900. Late last night our friends the Roughs (72nd I.Y.) received the order to return to Pretoria at once. So they left us this morning. And here are we, the Silly Sussex, still sticking to it, like flies on treacled paper. As Nobby says, "Grouse all day and you're happy. That's the way in the Army." He is quite right, and I am sure most of us Yeomen, myself unexcepted, have the true military spirit. For we really ought to be very good and contented in this charming valley, where, "if it were not for the kopjes and the snipers in between," we might lead a perfect Arcadian life. I shall miss our Roughs. Some of them are rare good fellows, and always cheery. To see a Rough come into camp after a good day's scouting on the farmhouse side of the valley, was a sight never to be forgotten. Across his saddle, *à la* open scissors, would be two large pieces of wood, usually fence posts; oranges dropping from his nose-bag; on one side of his saddle a fowl and a duck on the other; a small porker from his haversack; the ends of onions or such like vegetables would be protruding, and his broad-brimmed hat or bashed-in helmet would be garlanded with peach blossoms, resembling a joyous Bacchanalian, and the unshaven, dirty face underneath wreathed in smiles. We have destroyed a lot more waggons and houses, and lifted several hundred of cattle, besides getting some prisoners. How the women must hate us! Their faces are invariably concealed by the large sunbonnets which they wear, year in and year out. These articles of headgear have huge flapping sides, which their wearers apparently always use for wiping their eyes or noses with. This custom or fashion saves them a deal of time and trouble in fumbling for the usual inaccessible pocket. I daresay you have often read that the veldt is burnt by the Boers, to make our khaki visible on the black ground. More often than not a veldt fire is caused by accident, not design, a carelessly-dropped match doing the trick. As regards showing up our khaki, it is bad for dismounted fellows, but for the mounted men preferable to the sun-dried grass, for as nearly all our horses are bays, roans, chestnuts or blacks, they show up terribly on unburnt stuff and are almost invisible on the burnt.

Thursday, October 18th. We are very up-to-date out here, as the following will show you:

'Twas uttered in vast London city
By *lion comiques* without pity,
Provincial towns were not belated,
But showed they, too, were educated;
In many a rustic, quiet retreat,
Bucolics, too, would not be beat;
At last *It* crossed the mighty main,
Did Britain's latest great inane,
And we out here in deep despair,
Have been informed that *There is 'air.*

I am pleased to record that the beauty of this epoch-making remark and the evident subtle charm underlying it, has not yet dawned upon any of the troops with which I have come in contact, and so, apart from being aware of its existence, it has molested me in no degree. Even the Transvaal has its compensations. Look at the moral and intellectual damages one escapes—occasionally. Whiteing managed to get some rather good books at an untenanted house a few days ago. Byron's Complete Works, two Art Journal Christmas numbers (Burne-Jones and Holman Hunt), "Henry Esmond," and others. He gave me Henry George on "Progress and Poverty," and two or three works of a devotional nature. The latter I gave Nobby last night in the dark. Our conversations in the ranks are very diversified. A few days back we were arguing as to which is the better— a treacle pudding or a plain suet pudding with treacle. We were interrupted in the middle by a few snipers potting at us. This morning we stopped in the midst of a most interesting discussion on Aubrey Beardsley as a decorative artist and the influence of Burne-Jones and Japanese art on his earlier work, to kill fowls and loot eggs. Our bag was eight cacklers and six eggs—which have just proved to be, as I feared, addled. Lately we have had a really lazy time of it, the poor Infantry scouring the hills and we leisurely riding a few miles along the plain as advance or rearguard, and then camping by about mid-day.

The breaking up of the Composite Squadron.

Friday, October 19th. Yesterday evening the Devons and Dorsets were rejoined by their ex-policemen, over a hundred in number. They looked very fit, and appeared pleased to get on the column again. The Devons have their popular officer, Captain Bolitho, with them again. The Sussex did not turn up. However, they and the Somersets are expected to-morrow. As regards mails, we were not wholly disappointed. I got one batch of letters, bearing the home postmark of September 14th, also some newspapers. In one of the latter was a very florid four-column account by a famous "War Special," of the doings of Rundle's Starving Eighth. It included a picturesque description of one of those common occurrences, a veldt fire. "And now the flames roll onward with their beautifully-rounded curves sweeping gracefully into the unknown, like the rich, ripe lips of a wanton woman in the pride of her shameless beauty," and so on, at much length. I read Nobby portions of this article, but, alas! the hardy Parnassian mountaineer was too much for him. "Wot's it all about?" he queried, "I can't rumble to the bloke." I explained to a certain extent, for Nobby had been with the force in question. "Well, 'e can sling the bat," observed my Border friend, and we discussed and criticised various officers and the Army in general. The freshly-joined men brought with them nice new iron picketing pegs, which we who had long since lost or broken ours, eyed with covetous optics, and determined to possess later, if possible. Their lines were laid in a mealie field, and pulled-up pegs might well be expected. At midnight a clanking noise near my recumbent form, strongly reminiscent of our ancestral ghost, the dark Sir Jasper, dragging his clanking chain after him at that hour, as is his wont, aroused me. Of course, it was a horse which had pulled up his picketing peg and was searching for fresh fields or fodder new. I quickly grasped the situation and the peg, and now have no trouble when the pleasant words "'Smount. Pile arms. Off saddle. *Picket* and feed!" greet my ear.

Saturday, October 20th. Yesterday we returned towards Hekpoort, and the order for the day was "The Force will halt." Now this is one of the finest of life's little ironies which the Imperial Yeomen experience out here. "The Force will halt"—every time this cheerful intelligence is conveyed to us, we know we are in for something extra in the way of "moving on." To-day's "halt" has been a ten-mile halt, we having been ordered to proceed down the valley and guard a small bridle path across the Magaliesberg Range; Steyn, De Wet, or Delarey, being expected to try and get through at this particular point. The last time the Force halted, our halt was a 20 or 30 mile one to Bethanie. The time before a big patrol; and another halt consisted of a ride out several miles to open sundry graves which were suspected of being Mauser-leums, but were not.

Life on a Kopje.

BLOK KLOOF,
(About half-way between Hekpoort
and Commando Nek).
Sunday, October 21st, 1900.

Can it be the Sabbath? Last night I was in charge of one of the pickets on top of the already referred to kopje. The ascent of that kopje, oh dear! This morning I was sent on to another kopje directly in front of the one we had occupied during the night, to find out if an infantry picket was holding it. The going was too awful. As usual, the distance was greater than it looked, and only having had half-a-messtinful of coffee and a biscuit for breakfast on the preceding day, and a mouthful of half-boiled trek ox, which had to be gulped down before ascending the iniquitous hill in the evening, minus tea and water, I did not half appreciate the lovely sunrise and view which were to be seen gratis from the various summits. It was a long time before I got back to our little encampment (I slipped down on the rocks several times from sheer exhaustion), and found to my delight that coffee had been kept for me. I wolfed it all, the grounds not excepted, and, bar stiffness and, paradoxical to remark, a general feeling of slackness, was soon myself again. Our Sussex ex-Police, about fifty in number, are at another nek about a mile off, under Messrs. McLean and Wynne. Of course, they have not brought our mails; they managed to call for them when the office was closed. I was sorry to hear that a friend in the Devons (Trooper Middleton), who went into hospital the last time we were at Pretoria, has since died of enteric.

Monday, October 22nd. It really seems absurd giving days names out here! To-day, we Sussex men, who number about half-a-dozen, are being exempted from duty, as we expect to join our fellows who are at the other little pass. Once the various companies are re-formed, we shall be under a sort of new old *régime*. We are wondering anxiously what our fresh cooks will be like. The ones we have at present are not bad fellows; indeed, I call them Sid and 'Arry, which means an extra half-pannikin of tea or coffee. Yesterday afternoon we had a gorgeous thunderstorm, the lightning being incessant. I laid under some trees with a blanket and overcoat covering me, smoking, and with one hand slightly protruding, holding a *Tit-Bits* paper, which I read till it became too pulpy. A couple of our Sussex fellows have just ridden in; their lot strike camp and return as far as Rietfontein this evening, and so this letter goes with them.

Tuesday, October 23rd. Still at the same place. Yesterday, at about the identical hour as on the preceding day, a big thunderstorm came on us, but the comparison was as that of a curtain-raiser to a five-act drama, for yesterday's storm lasted well into the night, and drenched most of us thoroughly. When a few days ago we were ordered here, we were told to take only one blanket, and I, like most other fellows, stupidly obeyed and took a thin one, through which the rain comes as through a sieve. We were under the impression that our kit waggon would be sent after us, but oh dear no, that is eight miles back in Mr. Clements' camp. For kopje work Thomas A. gets extra rations and a daily rum allowance; we have been drawing less rations, and as for rum, ne'er a sniff o't. My overcoat is simply invaluable, and keeps me drier than some of the fellows. When you get wet out here, there is no one to come and worry you to be sure and change all your clothes, especially your socks. It would not do if there were, because, like the London cabbies, we never have any change!

* * * * *

Now the sun is shining, and our blankets and various raiment are drying, but it's 10 to 1 that about four we shall have a repetition of yesterday. Our present home is a veritable insect kingdom. Over, under and around us and our meagre belongings, crawl ants small, medium and big; bugs and beetles of all sects and denominations; all sorts and conditions of flies from the small pest to the tsezee view us with interest; as do also caterpillars and other centipedian and millipedian crawlers; wood lice and the domestic shirt ones, which, like the poor, we have always with us; spiders of all sizes, including tarantulas; and, in addition, lizards and rats, while on the kopje, baboons walk about chattering all sorts of unintelligible witticisms about us.

Wednesday, October 24th. As predicted, we got our thunderstorm all right yesterday evening. For about half-an-hour the lightning never seemed to cease flickering about and jagging through the clouds, but the rain was not so bad. This morning the Fifes are sending into Rietfontein for mails. I hope we shall get some. I am handing this in for the post. As we only came here for twenty-four hours, we are not well off for literature or writing paper, though I brought some of the latter in my haversack: hence these lines. We shall soon have been here a week. The last time we went out for three days we remained out six weeks. I am a wonderful scavenger now. You should see me pitch like a hawk upon a dirty and torn ancient paper or book. As a result of a morning's work in that line, I am luxuriously reclining on my overcoat and reading a *Spectator*, after which I shall regale myself on the lighter and less solid contents of *Tit-Bits*; later, I shall go round and swap them for other papers or magazines. A lot of us are dreadfully afraid of doing strange things when we get back to civilised life, such as asking for the "—— —— salt" at dinner, diving our hands or knives into the dishes *immediately* on their appearance and securing the best pieces after the manner of the Israelite priests with the hooks in the flesh-pots, commandeering fruit, fowls, eggs, or vegetables from our neighbours' gardens, wiping our knives and hands on our breeches or putties after a course, or a hundred other habits which have become so natural to us now. My greatest fear is that in a moment of absent-mindedness I shall, if tired, throw myself down on some cab rank where the horses are standing still and with my head pillowed on my arm and a foot twisted in a rein take a forty winks, so accustomed have I become to the close proximity of 'osses, waking and sleeping.

Thursday, October 25th. This time two months hence it will be Christmas, and it looks as if, after all, I shall be spending it out here "far from home," cheerfully grumbling like a true British soldier, while the waggon crowd and sergeants' mess are enjoying most of *our share* of the Christmas tucker and other luxuries which are sure to be sent out. And you away in dear old Merrie England in be-hollyed and be-mistletoe'd homes enjoying your turkeys, puddings, and all that goes to make Christmas the festive season of goodwill, when families and friends re-unite for a short while, and eat, drink, and gossip generally, will, I am sure, amidst the festival, pause now and again to think of the wanderers on the veldt, and more than likely toast them in champagne, port, sherry, elder, or orange wine. That is if we are not home. If we are, we shall show ourselves thoroughly capable of doing the above ourselves; and as for gossip, heaven help ye, gentles! I suppose the Christmas numbers are out already, with the usual richly-coloured supplements of the cheerful order, such as a blood-stained khaki wreck saying good-bye to his pard, or the troop Christmas pudding (I s'pose I ought to say duff) dropped on the ground. But a truce to all such thoughts, perhaps we shall get home after all, and again p'r'aps not.

Eleven thirty a.m. Have just had an awful shock to my nervous system. A sergeant has been up and served us out with the first Yeomanry comforts we have ever seen, much less had. Each of us has received a ¼-lb. tin of Sextant Navy Cut tobacco. For the present, I cannot write more, I am too overcome.

(Resumed.)

I feel more composed now. We have just been told that two cases of "comforts" were sent out to us, but have been rifled of their best contents; so farewell to condensed milk, sardines, jam, etc.

Last night I was on the kopje again. Paget or somebody else being reported as driving the Boers towards this range of hills (Magaliesberg) we were told to be specially vigilant. The night was as dark as Erebus, and my turn to post the relief came on at eleven, the post being about forty yards away from where we were sleeping, and the intervening ground a perfect rockery, the task of getting there was no particular fun. As I relieved the post every hour-and-a-half, I had four or five stumbling, ankle-twisting, shin-barking journeys. At about two we had the usual storm, and the accompanying lightning was most useful in illuminating me on my weary way. The descent of the kopje this morning was, I think, more fagging than the previous evening's ascent, though quicker as you can imagine. Then came the cause of my wrath. The Fifes, who went after mails, had

returned, and there were none for us—of course. However,
"Hope springs eternal in the Yeoman's breast."
Some more fellows have gone into Rietfontein to-day, and there is just the chance.

An hour ago I had a most necessary shave and wash. All the pieces of looking-glass in the possession of the squadron having long since been lost or reduced to the smallest of atoms, this operation has to be performed without a mirror, though now and again Narcissus-like, I catch a glimpse of my features in the soapy, dirty water.

Friday, October 26th. It rained all last night, and has hardly left off yet. I have not a dry rag to my name. Even my martial cloak is sopping, though the lining is what, considering all things, I might call dry. So sitting on my upturned saddle beneath a weeping (not willow) tree, on the branches of which my wet blanket is spread above my head, I am going to amuse myself by writing letters. We have a few tents here, but as it is fifteen to a tent, and asphyxiation is not a death we devoted band of five Sussex men have an inclination for, we are continuing our out-door life. Consequently, we are now sitting on our saturated haunches awaiting sunshine above, smoking our pipes, and wondering when the war will come to a genuine end. What a number of officers have gone home sick—of it! Our friends the Fifes are awfully good fellows, and the best managed Yeomanry Squadron I have seen out here. Yesterday evening we were guests at a little sing-song round their fire, and partakers of their hospitality in the way of hot cocoa. Alas, the rain speedily brought what promised to be an enjoyable evening to an end, and it was every man to his own tent, booby hutch, or cloak and blanket. I was actually the recipient of two letters and a parcel yesterday evening, thanks undoubtedly to a mistake somewhere or other. The making of a correct declaration of the contents of a parcel and their approximate value, as required by the postal authorities, and the sticking of the same on the parcel which is to gladden the heart of the man in khaki far away, is, I fear, a dangerous thing to do. Take, for example, a package, the contents of which are veraciously announced on the affixed slip as "Tobacco, cigarettes, chocolate, pipe, and shirt; value £1 10s."—your friend's chances of getting it are about 50 to 1 against; but the same parcel with the brief announcement "Shirt and socks; value 5s." would probably reach him some day. A Fife friend tells me he now and again gets a large medicine bottle of—well, what would it be for a Scotchman? well-corked and marked "Developing Solution."

Saturday, October 27th. Still at the above address. Nothing of note to record. Flies an awful nuisance on us and everything. Fellows would not believe that the jam ration has been so reduced in bulk by flies. Some people won't believe anything—fortunately I had my share first, and perhaps I did take a *leetle* too much. No news of possibility of getting home by Christmas or the New Year. I feel vicious, and somebody must suffer, so here goes.

N.B.—I hold the late Alfred Lord Tennyson partly responsible.

THE YEOMAN.

(Dedicated to the Fife, Dorset, Devon, Somerset, and Sussex Imperial Yeomanry Squadrons.)

"The War has grown flat, stale, and unprofitable as a topic for conversation."—*Extract from Editorial Notes in "Black and White," September 20th.*

> We came from many a town and shire,
>   From road, and street, and alley,
> And, filled with patriotic fire,
>   Around the flag did rally.
>
> For many thousand miles we sailed,
>   Till reached was Afric's strand;
> At Cape Town for some weeks we stayed,
>   Not yet on foeman's land.
>
> At last we got the word to move,
>   To join the fighting army;
> And so we left our peaceful groove,
>   With fighting lust half balmy.
>
> Away we marched o'er dusty ways,
>   Through spruit and blooming donga,
> For chilly nights and burning days,
>   With feelings ever stronger.
>
> We passed Milishy on the road,
>   And heard their imprecations
> Because they bore the Empire's load
>   Upon communications.

At last we joined Lord Roberts' force,
  And later we did sever,
And got attached to bold Mahon's Horse,
  For we go on for ever.
With Hamilton and Mahon we went
  Due east to wet Balmoral;
Where oh! an awful night we spent.
  What ho! the victor's laurel!
Then west we rode to catch De Wet—
  We thought 'twas now or never;
But he, in his particular way,
  And we, go on for ever,
To Rustenburg we went with Mahon
  The wily Boers to scatter;
Burnt many a farm and useful barn,
  And got—our clothes a-tatter.
Then later, we did join Clements,
  From him to part, oh, never!
For wars may cease, and wars commence,
  But we go on for ever.
We grumble, grumble, as we roam
  Beside the hills or river,
For troops we hear are going home,
  But we go on for ever.
We steal (we call it loot out here)
  The foeman's fowls and tucker,
And now and then we come off well,
  And now and then a mucker.
We've marched by night to catch the foe,
  Yet spite each bold endeavour,
Crises may come and crises go,
  But *this* goes on for ever.
At home, first China, then elections,
  Have claimed their keen attention;
Now football, crimes, and other things—
  The War they seldom mention.
Soon our nearest and our dearest
  Won't think our generals clever,
If we and this confounded War
  Keep going on for ever.

Sunday, October 28th. Last night we ascended Avernus again, and did the usual guard on the summit. Of course, we had some rain and its concomitants. Apart from that, and the circumstance of the sergeant-major of the Dorsets, who is 6-ft. 3-ins., and scales 15 stone, treading on my head in the dark in mistake for a rock, nothing of note occurred.

As regards the incident alluded to, it lends significance to my being occasionally referred to as "Peter," thanks to my suggestive initials, P.T.R. Hence it seems natural for me to be mistaken for a rock. Still, I trust these mistakes will not often happen.

On Monday (October 29th), Captain McLean, of rowing fame, and Lieutenant Wynne marched up to Blok Kloof with the ex-Policemen of the Sussex Squadron, and we, having first been paraded before Sir Elliot—who in a few kind words severed his connection with us, to our regret, as captain—rejoined our former comrades. The other squadron of the 7th Battalion of West Somerset Yeomanry, under Captain Harris, was left for duty at Rietfontein.

Colonel Browne (we were all pleased to hear of his promotion this month) having received orders to withdraw from the Kloof and rejoin Clements at Hekpoort, gave the order for us to be ready to march off at dusk. Soon after sunset, rain, which had been threatening all day, commenced to fall, and we had a rather uncomfortable night march to Hekpoort. We reached there at midnight, turned-in on the wet veldt for a few hours and were up again at four. That day we were rearguard and going in a south-westerly direction marched through Hartley's Nek (in the Witwatersberg) and encamped the other side.

Death and Burial of Captain Hodge.

On October the 31st we were right flank to Cyperfontein, and came in for the inevitable sniping. Mushrooms, which were very abundant on the veldt we were traversing, were collected by many of us, and on our arrival in camp cooked in a stew or fried in Maconochie bacon fat. We also came upon two Boer waggons under some trees, from which we obtained a huge loaf of mealie bread and some useful enamelled tin ware—likewise a basin of excellent custard. Several women thereupon came up from a house not far off and protested against our pillaging the waggons, as they only contained their property. "And their men?" we queried. They had none, knew nothing about any. A cock crowed in the neighbourhood, was located and promptly commandeered, and at the same moment, Boleno (not his real name) triumphantly emerged from one of the waggons with a fine pair of spurs and a quantity of tobacco; the simple Boer women had to accept us as unbelievers.

Further afield and unknown to us, the Fifes were having a warm time. It was only when we got into camp that we heard from our old friend, Sergeant Pullar, that their gallant and popular Captain (Chapell-Hodge of the 12th Lancers) had been severely wounded in retiring his men from a kopje to which they had advanced in scouting. He died the following night at Vlakfontein,* and was buried the next (Friday) morning.

As my horse had gone a bit lame, I was riding with the convoy that day, and so was able to wait and attend the funeral. I doubt the Fifes will ever forget that day

With *reveillé* rain began to pour in torrents. The advance and flanking parties moved out of camp, the Fifes had been told off for rearguard, on account of the funeral. Presently the convoy began to get under way with a lowing of oxen and cracking of whips, mingled with the bleating of captured flocks of sheep and goats. Standing under a tree beside my horse I waited; through the blinding rain I could see the ox teams by our Yeomanry lines swinging round in response to the niggers' shouts and whips, and with a gurring and creaking the waggons one by one took their place in the lengthy procession, disappearing in the dense atmosphere. One tent had been left standing, right and left of its entrance were drawn up the firing party and the rest of the squadron; leaving my horse I fell in with them. The sergeants presently emerged bearing on a stretcher, sewn up in the ordinary brown military blanket, the mortal remains of their captain. Then through the never-ceasing rain, splashing through pools of muddy water sometimes ankle deep, we slowly made our way to the back of a farm some

---

* It was this Vlakfontein which was destined to become notorious in the later history of the war. On the 29th of last May (1901), the 7th Battalion I.Y. lost heavily in a desperate fight at this place. Of the many gallant officers and men killed, all the members of the Battalion, past and present, must specially deplore the death of Surgeon-Captain Welford, one of the kindest and most self-sacrificing of men. Also Captain Armstrong, who joined the Battalion from Strathcona's Horse, as lieutenant, in November last. Lieutenant Pullar, writing to me in reference to the above, recently remarked: "It is the same Vlakfontein where the poor 7th Battalion lost so heavily in May, and I fear there must be many other graves there now."

fifty yards away, where at the feet of some huge blue gum trees, a grave had been dug. Several of the firing party who had no cloaks had their waterproof sheets over their shoulders, I noticed one man with a corn sack. Colonel Browne read the Service, the rain splashing on his little Prayer Book. The body was reverently lowered by means of a couple of ammunition belts from a machine gun, and the three rounds cracked strangely in the rain-laden air, the water dripping from the rifles. After the firing, one of the party, a dour-looking Scot, void of all sentiment I should have thought (God forgive me!) stooped, and picking some objects out of the mud, thrust them into a handy pocket. They were his three empty cartridge cases. Then the Fifes sorrowfully marched away, leaving their beloved captain behind them. Happy Fifes to have possessed so good an officer! Unhappy Fifes to have lost him!

* * * * *

Returning to where my poor saturated horse was miserably standing, I mounted and slowly rode along with the convoy. After going some miles, I was pleased to see the waggons turning off the slippery track on to the veldt and outspanning. Seeing close by the road, lying on the site of a former camp, sheets of corrugated iron from the roofs and other parts of a few wrecked and deserted houses in the neighbourhood, I dismounted and secured two large bent ones (these placed on the ground like an inverted V form excellent shelters for tentless men), and proceeded to carry them and drag my steed towards the camp. It was a long way and an awful fag. At length through the pelting rain, there bore down upon the Sussex Yeomanry lines two large bent sheets of galvanised iron, cursing horribly and followed by a dripping horse. Suddenly the sheets fell clattering to the wet ground and his comrades beheld the writer of these immortal letters. Whiteing, Boleno, and the rest of our special clique or mess, who had arrived before me had already commenced constructing Mealie Villas (being the name given to our family residence wherever we are). The ground was, of course, saturated by the rain, which continued unceasing all day. Huddled together in the cribbed, cabined and confined space of our "home, sweet home,"

CONSOLATION.

SUSSEX YEOMAN: "*It don't look like clearing off.*"

FIFE YEOMAN (*with chattering teeth*): "*I dinna care. It's juist the same or waur for them* (the Boers). *I hope they'll a' dee o' pneumonia.*"

half-naked, but fairly cheerful, we passed the time in everlastingly patching up the leaks and defects in the construction of the Villas. The next morning we had *reveillé* at six, and turned out promptly to feed the wretched horses; the poor, woe-begone looking creatures, hardly one of which was properly picketed, were standing expectantly amid a perfect cobweb of muddy, tangled picketing ropes in the quagmire, which represented their lines. One of the fellows, who had passed the night under our ox waggon, on lifting his rain-sodden blanket, found to his surprise and disgust a fine iguana, about four feet long, nestling against his body. The sun began to smile upon us, and we advanced to a better camping ground a few miles further on at Leeuwfontein. Here we outspanned and soon had our wet blankets, clothes, and other articles spread out on the veldt drying. The Force remained halted on Sunday, though we Yeomanry were sent out on a foraging patrol and returned with ducks and oranges galore. Late in the day, "Nobby," sallow, and with a week's beard on him, paid us a visit. He told us he had been bad and was dying, but bucked up at the sight of our rifles, which he pronounced as being in a disgustingly dirty state. "I'd like to be yer sergeant-major. I'd make yer sit up," quoth he indignantly, and then proceeded to give us the history of his own gun, and the godliness of its cleanliness. He also related to us portions of the history of the Border Regiment. "We're the Unknown Regiment," remarked Nobby, half bitterly, "but they ought ter know us now, we was with ole 'Art's Irish Brigade in Natal," and then came anecdotes of Pieter's Hill, and other places. Of course, he told us of their great marching feats, and wound up thus: "The other day Clements said to our ole man, 'Give the Borders a new pair of boots an' a ration of rum, an' they'll march to h——." Then after a pause, "Of course, that's a bit o' bunkum to keep us goin';" but his manner showed he was proud to repeat it nevertheless. On the 5th, we advanced to Doornkom, getting a fine herd of cattle from a kloof on our way, and having sundry necessary bonfires, principally of oat hay.

On Sunday (November 11th) we had some lively scrapping at the commencement of our march, which was towards Krugersdorp. During the day some of our Sussex fellows came upon an untenanted shanty, containing scores of packets of magnificent candles. They brought away all

On Pass

This depicts three of ours just going into the town — and the beauty & sadness of the whole thing is — they are got up to kill

they possibly could, and were very generous to the rest of us with them. That evening Mealie Villas was brilliantly illuminated, and later I had the pleasure of presenting

Dr. Welford and Captain Cory with a packet of these unobtainable articles. Another man who had been on a ration fatigue at the A.S.C. waggons in the afternoon managed to take away a box of four dozen tins of apricot jam, *not* down on our requisition. To "do" the A.S.C. is a virtuous deed. So we have dined well lately, though at the present time of writing I am rather tired of apricot preserve.

This day, Monday (November 12th), the column marched into Krugersdorp. We were rearguard and just as we left the site of the camp, which had been in a most picturesque spot, got bullets whistling by us and knocking up the dust round our horses. Two of our men out of four, who had relieved an infantry picket at *reveillé* are missing. The snipers followed us about half the distance to the dorp and we had quite a warm little rearguard action. I am just off to post this in the town.

Camp Life at Krugersdorp,

KRUGERSDORP,
Saturday, Nov. 17th, 1900.

We are still camped within about three miles of this town, and expect to remain here till Hart's Column returns. It went out yesterday after having had a five weeks' rest. Amongst the mounted men were the Wilts, Bucks, Yorks, and Suffolk Squadrons of Yeomanry. I think I told you in my last we arrived here on Monday after a lively time as rearguard, the Boers opening fire on us as soon as we had started to leave the place we had camped at. That is the worst of pitching upon picturesque spots for camps. We lost two men, who, however, eventually turned up safe and sound, although some of their captors had shown a strong inclination to shoot them, but, thanks to Delarey's brother, the bloody-minded minority were disappointed. The snipers hung persistently on to our tail, occupying each ridge and kopje as we retired from them. As soon as I had picketed and fed my horse, I obtained leave and went into Krugersdorp, passing on the way mines all the worse for want of wear, and the "Dubs" and others under canvas. In the town I dined at what I should imagine was a Bier

Halle in the piping days of peace, but which in the sniping days of war is an underground eating room run by Germans, who charge a great deal for a very little, and find it far more profitable than gold-mining.

I procured some tins of condensed milk, golden syrup, and jam for our larder, and volumes by Ruskin, Meredith, Thackeray, and Kipling, for my own somewhat small library. With these I proudly staggered back to camp, aware of the royal and well-merited reception which awaited me, and which I got. Whiteing was quite overcome at the sight of Ruskin and Thackeray, while another friend implored permission to have a dip in "The Seven Seas" (which seems a big request, I doubt not, to the uninitiated).

I forgot to mention that on my return to camp I found mails awaiting me. Thus passed a pleasant day. Tuesday I spent in camp, writing replies to my kind correspondents, reading and re-reading my letters and papers. We hear the C.I.V.'s are home, good luck to 'em, and though I have not read the papers I can imagine to a slight extent the enthusiastic welcome they were accorded. The knowledge that we have done our duty will be enough for us; never mind the brazen bands, the free drinks, the dyspeptical dinners, the cheers and jingo songs. Suffice it for us if you will let us quietly alight from the train and get us home, to our ain firesides. I fear I am rather bitter to-day; but, Christmas is coming, and the date of our return no man knoweth! On Thursday we all had to turn out to be inspected by "Bobs." If the turn out was to give him an idea of our strength as a fighting force the whole thing was "tommy-rot" for we paraded as strong as possible in numbers. The halt, sick and the blind, so to speak, were in the ranks, every available horse being used to mount them. Thus we turned out, our officers anxiously making the centre guides prove, and issuing special orders to us not to crowd when marching past in column of squadrons and all that sort of thing, Then we marched to the parade ground, cow gun, field guns, pom-poms, Infantry, Yeomanry, and Colonial mounted troops. After a short wait a group of mounted beings appeared in the distance and approached the force. We carried arms, and the infantry presented them. The great little man and his staff passed along the front of the force, and then cantered away, and the show was over, after having in all occupied about five minutes. In the way of guards and pickets we are not over-worked, the regiment having to supply a picket of one officer and twenty men every night, which means each squadron comes on every fourth night. The job is, also, what Tommy would call a distinctly "cushey" one.

On Friday I went into the town and succeeded in securing a fine stock of things for our larder, including a slab of Genoa cake, which I purchased at the Field Force canteen, which has just been opened. In the evening we entertained Sergeant Pullar, of the Fifes, at tea. This, though I should be modest over it, was really a grand, indeed sumptuous repast. Many a time has this gentleman given us biscuits on the veldt in our hours of need, papers also to read, and so we meant to do the thing well, and we did. In the morning a special invitation was sent from the corporals of the Sussex Squadron residing at Nos. 1, 2 and 3, Mealie Villas, requesting the pleasure of Sergeant Pullar's company to afternoon tea, parade order optional. We formed a table of biscuit boxes, which we covered with two recently-washed towels, and then I managed to obtain a fine effect in the way of table decoration by taking the spotted red handkerchief from my neck and laying it starwise as a centre-piece. Then, having begged, borrowed and otherwise obtained all the available tin plates, we covered the table with sardines, tinned tongues, pickles, condensed milk, jams, butter, and cake. Sergeant Pullar having arrived with his plate, knife, fork and spoon in a haversack, we sat down on S.A.A. Cordite Mark IV. boxes, to a rattling good feed, which guest and hosts did full justice to. Then it rained, and we had to rig up our blanket hutches in record time, while our guest sped to his tent. Thus ended an auspicious evening. The next morning we had the deluge, for it poured in torrents, our wretched blanket shelters proving far from rain-tight. But the real trouble was when we found we were being swamped, the water flowing in and sopping us and our belongings, the latter being by far the most important. Upon this I turned out and found the whole camp was a swamp, and all the shovels being used for digging trenches. Not to be done, I

118   A YEOMAN'S LETTERS.

collared a meat chopper from the Dorset cook-house, and started constructing trenches for all I was worth, specially draining my part of the villa where the library was

A Peep at our Domestic Life.

Tomkyns de Vere B.A. 'bucking up' the fire, Bolero Soles triumphantly approaching with more fuel, the district being a woodless one. While with a soul above cooking, but not eating, reading Marcus Aurelius in No. 1 Mealie Villas.

in great danger. The rain ceasing after a while, the other fellows emerged like so many slugs, and soon under my supervision (was I not articled to an architect once?) an elaborate system of drainage, consisting of trenches and dams, was constructed around the villas. We had a bit of a row with our neighbours, who complained that we had drained all our water on to them. A lot of unnecessary damming was indulged in. However, from our point of view the thing was a great success. Later the sun came out, and we dried all our possessions. Great institution the sun! The next day being the Sabbath, of course, we had to have a scrap, or at least try to have one. So we had a *reveillé* at 2 a.m., in order to surround a house where about forty Boers had been reported by some wretched being. On turning out, several of us found our horses had disappeared during the night, mine being among the number. So as not to be out of the fun, I took the first wandering brute I found, and fell in. All this took place in the dark, and later, when it became lighter, it was most amusing to see what some of us had secured. Mine proved to be an officer's charger, but no goer. When I got back to the lines, I found an infuriated officer's servant marking time in front of me till we were dismissed, when he approached and wrathfully spoke to me, stating that the horse had a sore back and was lame in three legs. As he gave me no chance to offer an apology or explanation, we slanged and abused one another for about ten minutes, to the delight of the squadron, and then parted so as not to miss other similar rows. The result of the morning's work was, I hear, two Boers captured. For this we all laid on the wet ground behind anthills and other cover for about two hours, waiting for them to come our way; while Legge's crowd pom-pommed and field-gunned them for about an hour. The Boers also used a good deal of ammunition, doing us no damage, but getting away through the usual missing link in the chain. This afternoon (Monday, 19th) we received mails, my share being three letters, and some papers.

Tuesday, Nov. 20th. I have just heard that we are off for a ten weeks' trek to-morrow, so I must bring this to a conclusion, and get into town to post it, and also to procure some more stores. It may or may not interest you to know that of all the jams we have had out here (and we have been served out with at least a score of different brands) the very best, made from the most genuine fruit, were the conserves of two Australian firms. These two firms are head and shoulders above all other makers bar none. "Advance, Australia" is right.

Well, here we are, and here we are going to remain, for how long the Fates only know. Sometimes in my most optimistic moments I cheerfully look forward to spending the golden autumn of my life in the land of my birth. As I write this evening by candlelight, in our rude substitute for a tent, I can hear the chorus of "The miner's (why not a yeoman's?) dream of home," which comes wafted to us from the Fife lines. As you will, I hope, receive this by Christmas, I take the opportunity to wish you and all kind friends a right merrie Christmas and a prosperous new year. For us no holly will prick nor mistletoe hang. If Santa Claus comes it will probably be with a Mauser, and for some, alas! obituary cards will take the place of the coloured productions of Bavarian firms. But come weal, come woe, where'er we be on that day, I can guarantee you our sentiments will be easily summed up by the following:

"Our heart's where they rocked our cradle,
Our love where we spent our toil;
And our faith and our hope and our honour,
We pledge to our native soil!"

Lady Snipers at Work.

KRUGERSDORP (again),
Wednesday, November 28th, 1900.

We returned here on Monday, after having been out for about a week's cruise on the troubled veldt, and, in spite of the rumour that we were to be treking again this morning, we are still here. I will endeavour to give you the usual veracious account of our doings. I say "veracious" advisedly, as oftentimes, after having seen something extra strong in the Ananias-Sapphira-Munchausen-Gulliver-de-Rougemont epistolary line from some gentleman in khaki to the old folks at home, in a London or provincial paper, I feel that I must give up letter writing altogether, as by now those at home must have discovered that such effusions are often seven-eighths lies, and the remaining one-eighth truth, simply because the scribe's powers of invention have failed him, owing to the great strain. Only yesterday I saw in a certain local paper such an epistle from one of our fellows, who, owing to various circumstances, only joined us in September last, and has now joined the estimable waggon crowd. From it I gathered that we had fought incessantly for several days, on one occasion being without food or water for thirty-nine hours, etc., and afterwards for our magnificent behaviour had been called up to the general's tent, warmly congratulated by him, and *presented with a pot of jam each*. So my diffidence about writing will be easily understood, I am sure. And now for the celestial truth.

On Wednesday last (November 21st) we had an unexpected *reveillé* at 1.30 a.m., and set out with four days' supplies for Somewherefontein (where, we did not know). A "revally" at such an hour is, as you may imagine, by no means devoid of interest; I don't know whether you have ever experienced one; if you have you know all about it; if not you have a great experience lacking. There was I, collecting and packing our larder in an oat sack, my miniature Bodleian and other various possessions in another, dismantling our blanket shelter, and a hundred other things, including feeding and saddling up my Rosinante, and then—"Stan' to your 'osses!" We paraded smartly, and after a short wait, moved off as right flank. A few hours after dawn there was fighting in front of the column, but not our way, Legge's crowd working on a parallel road and some way ahead of us. At about mid-day we reached a wonderfully fertile village (Sterkfontein), and, imagining it to be unoccupied, our Provost-Marshal and his satellites rode forward to select a site for our camp, and got well sniped from some of the houses. Thereupon Number Eight came up, and at comparatively speaking short range, opened fire and 15-poundered them. To us, who were watching the show, the sight was a most interesting one. Crash through a house would go one shell, another would account for something else, and flames and smoke soon announced burning thatches and oat-hay stacks. The Mausers soon ceased from troubling, and eventually we entered the fontein. To our surprise no snipers were captured, and it was asserted that the firing had been done by the ladies, who, with children, were the only persons found there. However, as no firearms or signs of their having done so, were found, the matter, like most things where the wily Boer is concerned, remains a mystery. It is a fact that lady snipers do exist. For some time the Borders had in their guard-room, during our last trip, amongst the various prisoners, a lady sniper they had bagged while doing the Magaliesberg. There was not much of the Jeanne d'Arc about her. I saw her once or twice. She was a regular barge, and of great beam; her face was concealed by the usual kindly sun-bonnet.

(*Note.*—Our Regimental Sergeant-Major has just gone by, with white canvas shoes and slacks on. This is most reassuring as regards not moving off to-day).

Well, we camped near the village, which lay in a sort of saucer, being surrounded by kopjes. On one of these our cow gun, yclept "Wearie Willie," was hauled; it took fifty-six oxen to get him up there. The Boers, whom we had surprised, were very sick at our unexpected visit, and, had they only known, would undoubtedly have attempted to hold the place a bit. As it was, they hung about far off. It rained a perfect deluge that night, and my blanket roof collapsing I went to sleep with it over me as it fell, lullabyed by the soft cursings of my neighbours of 1 and 2 Mealie Villas, who were in like plight. The next morning we were to have had *reveillé* at 5.30 and proceed to Rietfontein 12. (They have to number these places out here. You probably have noticed the innumerable Elandsfonteins, Hartebeestefonteins, Rietfonteins, Bethanies, etc., in the Transvaal and Orange River Colony.) But Brother Boer willed it otherwise, and about an hour before the fixed time I was "revallyed" by the banging of guns distant and near. I arose to my feet and the fact that Mr. Delarey was trying to shell us, as a not far distant crack of an exploding shell testified. Near me, from under a rain-soaked blanket a sun-bronzed face appeared and a sleepy voice inquired "are the *burchers* (burghers) shelling us?" The seeker after knowledge was informed they were. We soon got the order to turn out, saddle up and escort the guns. This we quickly did. As we moved out a few shells skimmed over the kopjes and lobbed themselves where our lines had been. By this time our field guns and cow gun were well at it, and the Boers were shifting a bit. We dismounted, lined the kopje we had ridden up to, and watched the work of our gunners. Presently from half up the hill in front of us, I saw a flickering white flash and pom-pom-pom-pom-pom-pom went Delarey's gun of that name, followed by a whistling over our heads and half-a-dozen cracks behind, where, looking round, I saw the same number of puffs of smoke and earth arise from the ground. This went on for a while, they were trying to get on our led horses, I believe. I afterwards heard some went fairly close, also that the general had one very near. *Apropos* of this pom-poming, our colonel, who had had their missiles all round him and had quite ignored them, as is his invariable custom, strolled up to one of our officers and the conversation turning on to pom-poms, languidly remarked: "Ye-es, I don't think they do much weel destwuction—er-er —it is pwincipally their demowalising effect." The demoralising effect on himself having been so very non-evident, this remark struck me as being distinctly good. Our "Wearie Willie" snapped out a remark now and again, and apparently always to the point. Later, Legge's men occupied the ridge opposite and chivvied the enemy for several miles; we, returning to camp, watered our horses and, twenty minutes later, set out on a reconnaissance with the guns in hopes of finding some snipers in the vicinity of Hekpoort. We returned bagless. That night it rained, as usual, and as we had not had time to rig up any shelters, or even dry our blankets, we came in for another good wetting. At two o'clock the next (Saturday) morning we had to turn out and stand to our horses. "Steady, boys, steady, we always are ready"—*afterwards;* you know our good old British style. But Frater Boer had had a belly full the preceding day, his losses in killed and wounded being considerable, I hear. Legge's men swear to have buried eight, and Clements said one of our shells hit a gun of their's. That night we had the fashionable and seasonable rain again (Please, in future, remember we have this every night, and so I will refrain from too many references to it). On Sunday we moved off for Rietfontein, No. 1001. We formed the rearguard and expected a bit of harassing, the country being most favourable for such operations on the part of the enemy. But they left us alone, though they were undoubtedly about unseen. As several waggons broke down, and had to be mended or burned, we had to grill on the kopjes for hour upon hour, cursing the convoy with all our might. Presently the inevitable question "What's the date?" elicited the fact that it was the 25th. (You can imagine the chorus "A month to Christmas!" and Sunday.) Sunday, and you probably in your frock coat and patent boots, luxuriously reclining in an upholstered pew, listening to promises of peace and rest, or standing up half thinking of the good meal to follow, and singing

"I came to Jesus as I was,
Weary, and worn, and sad;
I found in Him a resting place,
And He hath made me glad."

And I, there on those hard rocks, with a perpendicular sun above me, mechanically watching the distant hills, but seeing with strong mental eyes a church porch with roses and creeper over it and noting the Sabbath silence which presently would be broken softly by the voices of the worshippers within:

"Come unto Me, ye weary,
And I will give you rest."

I think to stand outside a church and hear the worshippers within is to get one of the most pleasant impressions possible; somehow it always strikes me that one imagines the people within to be so much holier, indeed more spiritual, than they really are. But all this looks either like preaching or scoffing, and it is neither. It is really the result of a desire to push myself into the home life you good people are still leading, somehow or other. An excusable offence after all, my Masters! Having re-cursed the tail of the convoy, it at last moved forward, and we, having allowed it so much grace, did the same. At the outskirts of the village, which the column had moved through, the last waggon—an overloaded one—collapsed, and once again we manned the heights. I was sent out with a couple of men to a post a little in advance of the rest of our troop, and, after an hour, about a mile off saw four Boers nonchalantly riding toward the other side of the dorp. These were followed by two more. I sent in and reported this, and shortly after we moved off, unsniped. Undoubtedly these beggars had been waiting for the column to pass, so that they could return and have a Sunday dinner and a quiet evening, having had rather a rough week, and it was only owing to the above-mentioned waggon breaking down that we had a glimpse into the ways of our enemy. Our camp was not far off, and we go there at about six; some of the column were in by eleven in the morning. The amount of burning done *en route* was almost appalling. The next day we marched into Krugersdorp once again, passing several marshy spots where arum lilies were blooming in rich profusion. We reached here at noon; the Dorsets and Devons who formed the rearguard had a bit of scrapping, and, thanks to a straggling convoy, did not get into camp till close on midnight, and so, of course, got a rare soaking from the usual rain. Here I have received a few belated mails, and live in hopes of getting the latest. I have also read in some of the papers of the welcome home of the C.I.V.'s.

> "You've welcomed back the C.I.V.'s,
>   Back from their toil to home and ease;
> The war is going pretty strong,
>   *We've* bade adieu to 'sha'n't be long';
> And you at home across the seas,
>   Don't quite forget *us*, if you please."

The following poetic outburst requires a little explanation. We have had the khaki this and the khaki that, and it has just occurred to me a khaki Omar Khayyam would not be out of place, for of a truth one needs a *soupçon* of philosophy out here occasionally. With this idea in my head, and having a little leisured ease, I have set out to minister a long-felt want. Not, however, having my Persian "Fitzgerald" by me, I must ask your indulgence for any grave discrepancies in the text.

THE RUBAIYAT OF OMAR KHAYYAM.
(For the use of British Soldiers on the Veldt.)

> The night has gone, the golden sun has riz,
> The khaki men have all begun to friz,
>   Cleared is the mushroom camp of yesterday,
> And forth they go upon the Empire's biz.

Oh! hopes of home that with each morning rise,
Oh! wondrous legends which wild minds devise;
   One thing is certain, and the rest is lies,
The Yeoman, once enlisted, often sighs.

Oh! fool to cry "The Boer is on the run,"
He is, we know, and *ain't forgot his gun;*
   And often from the rocky kopje side
He stops and pots——your mess is minus one.

I sometimes think that nought whiffs on the wind
As strong as where some dying steed reclined;
   That any casual stranger passing by
The place, if asked, again could eas'ly find.

Alas! that Mausers are not turned to hoes,
That Christmas comes, and with the pudding goes;
   And we stick here for ever and a day,
When we return (or *if*) *who knows*—WHO KNOWS?

Oh! Pard, could thou and I with Holmes conspire
To round De Wet up with his force entire;
   Would we not smash it all to bits—and then
Get somewhere nearer to our heart's desire.

A pipe o' baccy 'neath a leafy tree,
A recent mail from far across the sea,
   No one to worry for an hour or two,
And veldt, indeed, were Paradise to me.

And, lo, 'tis vain the generals to blame,
Keep boldly sticking at the ancient game;
   And if to-day you are upon the veldt,
To-morrow it will also be the same.

Each morn's *reveillé* comes like some nightmare,
Sleepy you rise and pack your kit, and swear;
   Then mount your saddled steed with gun in hand,
And hasten off, you know not why or where.

Some in the fighting let their hearts rejoice,
For some the waggons are the patriot's choice:
   Oh! loot the farm, don't let the chickens go,
Nor heed the roaring of the sergeant's voice!

They say the gentlemen in khaki keep
The courts where Kruger once did plot so deep;
   That great Oom Paul across the sea has trekked,
Before the Courts of Europe now to weep.

We are but pawns, first front, then flank, then rear,
Moved by the Master Players there and here
   Upon the veldt and kopje (that's the board),
Sans tents, *sans* beds, *sans* pudding and *sans* BEER.

> Yon broiling sun which smiles and is our bane,
> Yon thunder-cloud which means a soaking rain,
>   Will both some day look down upon this veldt
> For us, and let us hope 'twill be in vain.

The above extract will, I am sure, suffice to show the general tone of the khaki Rubaiyat, and be more than enough to damn my poor but honest reputation.

Treatment of the Sick.

KRUGERSDORP,

December 5th, 1900.

As the English mail leaves this benighted place to-morrow at mid-day, I am dropping you a few lines, though I feel in anything but a scribbling humour. Clements moved out on Monday for about a week's jaunt, and left us, the Sussex Squadron and sick men, behind in charge of about a hundred remounts, mostly Argentines; and with the pleasant task of doing pickets and such like, about two miles out from the town. As I write I am very wet, it having been raining for the last two days. This morning the other four occupants of Mealie Villas had to clear off at 3 o'clock to do a picket, and so, as they naturally withdrew the support of their rifles from their blankets, there was not much shelter for me. I wonder what your opinion was on the statements of Mr. Burdett-Coutts, M.P., as regards certain hospitals out here, and also what you think of the Army doctor? It was my duty to parade the sick men before one of these august beings this morning. I received the order at a quarter past nine from our Squadron Sergeant-Major to parade before the doctor's tent, in the lines of Marshall's Horse, at 9.30. So at that time, behold me with fourteen sick men in the driving, drenching rain waiting in puddles of water outside the well-closed tent of the disciple of Esculapius. There we waited till at last an officer entering the tent, in response to my inquiry, as to whether I was at the right place or not, replied in the affirmative and informed an unseen being that there was a sick parade outside. Apparently without even rising, the great unseen was heard to remark shortly, " Sick parade is at seven o'clock every morning," the tent was again closed, and the men with fever, dysentery, colds and sores wended their ways through the rain and mud, back to the damp interiors of their leaking blanket hovels. They were men of the Fife, Devon, Dorset, and Sussex Yeomanry Squadrons, and that is how some of your dear patriotic volunteers get treated occasionally by certain doctors out here. Our Battalion doctor (the 7th) is a very good sort, and if you are bad will see you at almost any time.

On Wednesday (November 29th) a friend and I went into the 'Dorp and got a few stores (alas! the Field Force canteen is almost empty and the prospects of its being replenished are drear). Afterwards we strolled up to the station to see if there were any mails, and to see a train again. The Johannesburg train came in while we were there, and a sergeant-major of Kitchener's Horse shot an officer of the same corps soon after alighting from the train. The officer had put him under arrest for misbehaviour in Johannesburg. I had my choice of a dozen yarns as to the real cause of the tragedy. The officer was buried the next day. The fate of the sergeant-major I have not heard yet, though it is not difficult to guess. Mr. Wynne, our troop leader left us this day for England, having applied for leave on business. A statement of the losses among our officers may not be uninteresting. All of the following, save the last, are home or on their way: The Duke of Norfolk, injured thigh; the Hon. T. A. Brassey, elections; Mr. Ashby, reasons unknown, but undoubtedly excellent; Mr. Williams-Wynne, business reasons; Mr. Cory, still out here but working with the transport—hard.

Which leaves us Mr. McLean, of rowing fame, as our captain and only officer.

Saturday, apart from lifting us into December, was I believe, uneventful.

Veldt Church Service.

On Sunday we had a Brigade Church Service—we had not had one for a long time. We also had a real padre, who wore a surplice, cassock, and helmet, and who preached an indifferent sermon. I don't suppose we deserve a real good man.

Hymns & their Singers
(At an I.Y. Veldt Church Service.)
"I was not ever thus." Lead kindly Light.

The great event of Tuesday was the fate of my Christmas pudding, which I had received from my *Mater*. Having handled and examined it carefully for some time, I thought I could detect signs of decomposition about it. I communicated my fears to my comrades, who shared them, and said they didn't think it would last till Christmas. It didn't; for we ate it that evening. It was good, and I suppose we ought to feel ashamed of ourselves for eating it out of season, but really our excuses are many, principal among them being it is not wise trying to keep edibles, as they have a way of getting lost, and if the pudding managed to last to Christmas it is just on the cards we might not.

To show you how civilised we are at the 'Dorp, we, when in standing camp, occasionally have a chance of getting a drink of beer. This afternoon a barrel was brought into our camp, and to-night we shall be able to buy pots of it at sixpence a pint. You should see those pints! We may be Imperial Yeomanry, but they don't give us Imperial Pints. Teetotalers will be interested and pleased to hear that out of our princely stipend of 1s. 3d. per diem (unpaid since July) we don't buy much of the beverage.

I have drawn a fresh horse from the re-mounts we are in charge of; my last gee-gee I called "Barkis," because he was willing, this brute I shall have to dub "Smith," because he certainly is not—Willing.

N.B.—Our mounts are always known as "troop horses," those belonging to the officers though, however Rosinante-like, are invariably, politely and with dignity alluded to as "chargers."

Thursday morning. We had to turn out and stand to arms this morning at three, an attack being expected on the railway. I, happening to have the stable picket, had the pleasure of arousing the recumbent forms of the sleepers with the joyous Christmas carol of "Christians, awake! come, salute the happy morn." You ought to have seen the "Christians" awake; to have heard them would have been too awful.

So from three till six we stood to arms, a thick fog enveloping us, making it impossible to see more than fifty yards to our front or rear. But they did not come. I understand that we may have "the stand to arms" wheeze every morning now, so we have something to look forward to.

Comradeship.

KRUGERSDORP.

Wednesday, December 12th, 1900.

As we are under orders to leave here and join Clements to-morrow, I am writing so as to catch the mail which goes out on Thursday.

On Sunday we had a Church Service, and in the afternoon had a visit from Nobby—the Border Regiment has been resting at Krugersdorp for a few weeks—who entertained us till, what out here we should term a late hour, about nine.

On Monday I heard that another of our Sussex fellows had died of enteric at Pretoria.

Nobby has just looked in again, he is rather a swell, wearing one of our new war hats we had served out, and which I gave him, preferring to keep my old one; in his words, he looks as if he belonged to the "Yeomandry." It is wonderful how all our fellows get on with our professional brethren. Take for instance one of our men, a 'Varsity man, hight Pember, he is a dry, self-contained beggar, and lives his own life. Into this life has come a man of the Northumberland Fusiliers. They both hail from the same county. After the day's march, when the Infantry not on picket are in camp, a dark figure often slouches up our lines, and a voice inquires, "Is Pem 'ere?" and Pember of ours, late of Trinity Hall, calls out from the darkness, "Here you are, mate," and forthwith the man of the Fighting Fifth and the Imperial Yeoman sit down together and chat of Heaven knows what, and the latter gives the former half of his prized hard tack ration (he wouldn't give me a biscuit for his soul's salvation), for the Northumberlands do not fare well at their quartermaster's hands, at least they did not the last time we were on the trek. Then, at about the same time Nobby is leaving us, the Fusilier also arises and disappears with a "Good night, chummy," into the darkness.

The dry canteen, for the troops, in the town, is now quite empty. Fortunately, we still have some of the Great Candle Loot left, otherwise we should be very much in the dark after sunset. To save our candles from draughts and get a good light, we always burn them in biscuit tins, a practice I can recommended highly if ever you go out campaigning and lack a lantern. A convoy going to Rustenburg from Pretoria was attacked and part captured a few days ago by Delarey's crowd. I had expected that to happen soon, the length of the convoy and insufficiency of its guard, having frequently struck me as very tempting for Brother Boer.

Well, I must conclude, as I have nothing of note to narrate, and must begin to pack my possessions in a manner to circumvent our quartermaster-sergeant when packing our kits on the waggon.

IN HOSPITAL.

> IMPERIAL YEOMANRY HOSPITAL,
> PRETORIA.
> *Tuesday, December* 18*th*, 1900.

Dulce et decorum 'tis to bleed for one's country, especially to a small extent, and that is my case. So here I am taking my ease with a slightly stiff leg, caused by a flesh wound acquired during a lively rearguard action we had on the 14th, and my hand tied up in a manner to render writing rather a slow and fumbling ceremony. I always find it easier to write of the present than the past, so will get through the events of last week as quickly as possible. On Thursday last we left Krugersdorp for Rietfontein to join Clements, with the Borders, some mounted details and useless remounts. Half of our fellows were leading the latter. We, the remainder, formed the rearguard, and a long, wearisome job it was. Oh, how those waggons broke down and stuck in dongas and spruits! At last we got into camp, to my infinite relief, for the sun had, for once, given me a vile head. All through the day we heard guns firing, first near us and then distant. The next day we were again rearguard, and had a rare harassing. The end of that beastly convoy seemed to lag even more than on the preceding day! And we of the rearguard, on the kopjes and ridges, watched the enemy galloping round and up to the favourable positions, potting at them when we had a decent chance. But they knew the lay of the land, of course, and the closer they got the more invisible they became. They don't require khaki to make them indiscernible. Then a single shot would inform us as it hummed above our heads that one gentleman had got into position, and was getting the range, then others, and we knew his friends were with him, and hard at it. Once a few of us happened to be lying in front of a ridge we were holding, and *at which* the Boers were potting from another about 800 yards off. We got the order to retire over the crest and get better cover and had a warm time doing it. One at a time we crawled, then, crouching low, rushed back a few yards and dropped behind a rock for breath and cover. Then back again we dragged ourselves till the cover was better. Their firing was distinctly good, and several fellows were hit. On one occasion I dropped behind a small piece of rock, ostrich-like, covering my head, and almost simultaneously with my action a bullet struck the side of the rock a few inches from my face with a nasty *phutt*. That is what it is like on such occasions. That's the sort of game we played all day, cursing Clements for not sending out to meet us and give us a hand. We did not know what had happened in the valley the preceding day. Later we got into an ambush, some of the enemy being within a hundred yards of us; and had several horses killed. We thought that the show was over, as Rietfontein was close handy, and the last time we were there the locality was clear. It was almost dark when we entered Clements' camp. But where were the tents, the men and horses that used to be? Presently a figure with a face rendered unrecognisable by bandages, came up to us. It was Sergeant Pullar of the Fifes, and from him we had the story of the previous day's disaster. Over half the Fifes are missing, most of the Devons also, so-and-so killed, and so-and-so, and so-and-so. Kits lost, and tents burnt. From various reliable sources I have compiled the best account I can make of the affair, which we missed by the merest fluke, what men call chance, and here it is.

The Story of Nooitgedacht.

Clements' camp was at Nooitgedacht, between Hekpoort and Olifant's Nek, where he had been for three days. Nooitgedacht is at the base of the Magaliesberg range of hills (the name means "Ne'er Forgotten"). We had camped there about a couple of months back. It lies near a large kloof. A little to the west of Clements were Colonel Legge's mounted troops, composed of Kitchener's and Roberts' Horse, "P" Battery R.H.A., and two companies of M.I., the whole force numbering, at the most, 1,400 men. Knowing that Delarey was in the vicinity with a strong force, the general had helio'ed for reinforcements, which, unfortunately, were not forthcoming, so apparently he was sitting tight, with doubled pickets, on the Magaliesberg and kopjes in the valley. Then came the eventful Thursday (the 13th). During the night Beyers' Commando made a wonderful trek from the north to reinforce and co-operate with Clements' old foe, Delarey, and just before dawn the enemy, who had crept up unseen or heard in the dark, rushed Legge's pickets on the west of the camp, shooting the sentries and many of the men as they lay asleep in their blankets, soon afterwards getting into the gallant Colonel's camp. Poor Legge, who ran out in the direction of the pickets as soon as he heard the firing, was one of the first killed. Then Clements' pickets on the Magaliesberg, which were composed of four-and-a-half companies of Northumberland Fusiliers, suddenly became aware of the close proximity of the enemy, who were in great force, about 3,000, and had, undetected, crept up the gradual sloping northern side of the range. The Northumberlands soon exhausted their ammunition, volunteers of the Yorkshire Light Infantry tried to take them a fresh supply, but were allowed to toil up the steep hillside with their heavy loads, only to be dropped, when near their goal, by their exultant foes. Probably never before have the Boers fought with such boldness, standing up and firing regardless of exposing themselves. Meanwhile, the Yeomanry, who had been standing to their horses in the camp, received the order to reinforce the Northumberlands on the Magaliesberg above them, and, with the Fifes leading and Devons following, commenced to ascend the precipitous hillside. Alas, the Boers were in possession of the summit, the Fusiliers having surrendered, and the Yeomanry got it hot. Of the Fifes, Lieutenant Campbell, who had only joined them a fortnight ago at Krugersdorp, was the first to fall, struck by an explosive bullet in the head. Out of less than fifty, fourteen were killed, and almost all the survivors wounded more or less seriously. At last, without a ray of hope, they were compelled to surrender, too. Many a good comrade's fate is known to me, so far, by that direly comprehensive word, *missing*. I have heard that the Boers threw many of the wounded over the precipitous southern side of the Magaliesberg, but do not believe it. Then they turned their full attention to the camp below; every officer of the staff was hit, the brigade-major was killed, having many wounds. Clements himself went unscathed; wherever there was a hot corner the general was to be seen coolly giving orders and apparently unconcerned amid a hail of bullets. "I'll be d——d if they shall have the cow-gun," he remarked, and, by gad, they didn't. With drag ropes it was moved down the hill for some distance, and then an attempt was made to inspan the oxen. As fast as one was inspanned it was shot, and quickly another and another would share its fate. At last, by sheer desperate perseverance, some sort of a team was inspanned and the gun moved forward, leaving dead and wounded men and considerably over half of the ox-team behind, but with the aid of the field artillery, who shelled the kopjes, was at length got on to a comparatively safe road. Of a truth, were I another Virgil and a scribe of verse, not unheroic prose, I might well have started this little account with

"I sing of arms and of heroes."

The getting away of the transport was a desperate affair; the niggers scooted, and amid the roar of the field guns, pom-poms, maxims and rifles, which between the hills was terrific, the mules stampeded. Officers, conductors and troopers rode after the runaways, and, under threats of shooting if they didn't, compelled the niggers to return with the mules. Chief amongst the Yeomanry who distinguished themselves that day, was Sergeant Pullar, who rode after the retiring convoy, called for, and returned with volunteers to the camp and helped with the guns and ammunition, and in various other ways. At last the Boers swarmed into the camp and our guns, turning on it, shelled it, containing as it did, friend and foe alike, a regrettable but absolutely necessary measure. Then our force retiring down the valley to Rietfontein fought a fierce rearguard action, the Dorset Yeomanry under 'Sir Elliot Lees and the remnants of the Fifes and Devons forming the rear screen, supported by Kitchener's and Roberts' Horse, mostly dismounted, and the guns. During this retirement, which I have heard wrongly ascribed to the M.I., Sir Elliot and his orderly, Ingram, of the Dorsets, on one occasion finding that two dismounted Yeomen had been left behind on a recently abandoned kopje, gallantly rode back and bore them away on their horses into comparative safety.* The artillery were grand, as ever, and in spite of killed and wounded gunners and great losses in the teams, saved their guns and used them to effect. At six o'clock on Friday morning the rearguard entered camp at Rietfontein. Our casualties—killed, wounded and missing, are 640, while it is stated and believed that the enemy's losses were even more severe. It seems a strange coincidence that exactly this time a year ago at home in dear old England we were going through the black Stormberg and Colenso week, and Christmastide was coming to many a sorrowing home.

Since writing the above, I have heard vague tales that a good many of the missing have turned up at Rustenburg, being either men who got through or released prisoners. This I rather anticipated and hope to be true. About the Yeomanry I have not heard any reassuring news yet; one thing is certain—they had many casualties and fought desperately.

NOOITGEDACHT.

Thursday, December 13th, 1900.

Comrades of Fife and of Devon,
   Dying as brave men die,
Under God's smiling blue heaven,
   Now you peacefully lie
On the hills you died defending,
   Or veldt where you nobly fell,
Your foemen before you sending;
   Good comrades, fare thee well.

O comrades of Devon and Fife,
   Memories flood me o'er;
Fierce mem'ries of many a strife
   In days that are no more;
Full many a fast have we shared,
   Of many treks could I tell;
Brave men who have done and dared,
   Comrades of mine—farewell.

---

* For his share in this gallant deed, Ingram was promoted by the C.-in-C. to Corporal. Several of the Devons and Fifes were subsequently mentioned in despatches. Sergeant Pullar was persuaded to accept a commission, as also were Sergeant-Majors Gordon and Cave. All three being excellent soldiers and popular with the men. A Yeoman told me lately, "It was simply splendid the cool way in which Colonel Browne and Sir Elliot Lees superintended the waggons being moved from camp."

L'envoi.

And when in the great Valhalla
All of us meet again;
Norsemen in skins and armour
And men in khaki plain;
With a smile to erstwhile foemen
Who 'gainst us fought and fell,
I'll haste to my fellow Yeomen,
Till then, dear chums—farewell!

Two Field Hospitals—A Contrast.

On Friday I went before our Battalion doctor, who had lost everything, save what he stood in. However, he fixed up my leg and hand and exempted me from duty. On going before him the next day he said my leg wanted resting, and in spite of protests sent me to the R.A.M.C. field hospital. A word aside here. I suppose you have heard of this great institution of the British Army—the d——d R.A.M.C. (I seldom, if ever, have heard it alluded to without the big, big D's.) My experience of it, I am pleased to say, has been, so far, severely limited, but, slight as it is, I can quite understand why it is lacking in popularity. With three other Yeomen and my kit, I accompanied the doctor's orderly to the Brigade Hospital. The order for our admission was given in, and we were told we should be attended to at nine. The sun was hot, shade there was none, and outside the doctor's tent we waited. Nine came and went, a doctor also rode up, chatted with someone inside, and rode away. The sun was scorching, and we dare not go away to get in any friendly shade. Three of us had game legs and one dysentery, but, of course, we grumbled not, for the R.A.M.C. are all honourable men. Various squads of sick Artillery, M.I. and other regiments marched up, and finally an R.A.M.C. sergeant came to the entrance of the tent and began calling them up before the doctor. Eleven o'clock came, and in the hot sun we waited still, in spite of being half-determined to return to our lines, as it was getting rather wearisome and confoundedly hot; but the R.A.M.C. are all honourable men. A Canadian helped a chum down to the group of impatient patients, and after a few words left him with the terribly audible remark, "So long, ole man. I'd sooner blanked-well die on the veldt than go there." Which showed how he failed to appreciate the R.A.M.C., and also his bad taste, for those inside must have heard him. But there, they know that they, the R.A.M.C., are all honourable men. "Driver Neads!" calls the spic and span little dark-moustached sergeant, reading from a list of names. A ragged dirty-looking Artilleryman limps painfully up, *two pills* are given to him, he gazes curiously at them, then at the back of the donor, who has turned away, and then realising that nothing further is to be done for him, limps heavily back, making room for the next patient. Once in the background, he heels a small hole in the earth, turns the contents of his hand into it, methodically fills the hole up, and hobbles back with his squad. They were, of course, the celebrated "Number Nines," the great panacea out here as, of course, you know. They (are supposed to) cure all diseases, from dysentery and brain fever to broken legs and heads.

And still we, who were first, waited in the blazing sun, to be last. Finally the smart sergeant smilingly recognised us, and cheerily told us that there was an Imperial Yeomanry Field Hospital somewhere in the vicinity, and we were to go there, and with that returned us our admittance form. I pressed him for more accurate information, and had the supposed direction given me, which proved correct. So off we crawled, I, with my Bunyan's Pilgrim-like load, holding the position of a scratch man in a race. I could not have done the distance had I not procured the services of a nigger, who relieved me of my kit for a shilling. So we shook the dust of the R.A.M.C. Field Hospital from our boots, but let not an abusive word be levelled at them, for are they not all honourable men?

The Imperial Yeomanry Field Hospital was about a mile off, and on reaching it we were treated with every kindness. They had only come in the previous night, and we were the first patients. Every consideration was shown to us, and in a few minutes we were lying down in a fine tent of the marquee brand and drinking excellent *café au lait* and eating bully and biscuit. "The best we can do for you at present," as they apologetically remarked to us. Fomentations were applied to our wounds, and luxuriously reclining on my back, smoking a Turkish cigarette one of the orderlies had just given me, I fervently swore that the grandest institution in South Africa was the I.Y. Field Hospital. In the afternoon some sick Inniskilling Fusiliers were admitted, and for some time seemed dazed at the kind treatment they were receiving, and appeared half under the impression they were in Heaven. "What's this chummy?" queried one. "Imperial Yeomanry Hospital" was the reply. "Thank Gawd 'taint the R.A.M.C." grunted the Tommy, turning over on his side with a sigh of relief. At about ten that night we had to make room in our tent for a dozen wounded men from Thursday's fight. Ninety were being brought into Rietfontein and the I.Y. people were taking half. Soon an ambulance was halted by our tent, and wounded men hobbled or were carried in, heads, arms and legs tied up, with here and there blood showing through the bandages. They were M.I., Kitchener's Horse, Northumberlands and K.O.Y.L.I. (King's Own Yorkshire Light Infantry). "Man," started a Yorkshire man before he had been in the tent a minute, "they (the Boers) treated us real well." "Ay, they was all right," chimed in a M.I. man, "they gave us to eat as much as they 'ad." "One bloke arsked my permission to take the boots orf one of our dead chaps," said a Northumberland Fusilier. And at it they went hammer and tongue, especially the latter. To follow the various speakers one needed a dozen pairs of ears at least. Several related that the Boers came up to them and told them they had made a grand fight of it. They were quickly supplied with beef tea and biscuits, and some of the necessary cases were dressed again. "See that that man has a ground sheet down there," ordered Major Stonham, "he is on the bare earth." "I've laid on it for three nights out there, sir," cheerfully vouchsafed the patient under notice.

At last I got to sleep, awaking at four, and having had a small bowl of porridge and milk, arose with the other fellows who had come in with me and the sick Inniskillings, and getting our kits, got into an ambulance waggon for the first time. The I.Y. people sent in two ambulances and the R.A.M.C. three open mule waggons filled with sick soldiers. We reached Pretoria at three, and we four Yeomen were sent to the Imperial Yeomanry Hospital, where, after once again giving in our names, regimental numbers, ranks, regiments, service, ailments, religion, and a hundred other items of general information, I was allotted a ward, bed, and suit of pyjamas, and after having had a bath, got into bed and awaited the next person desirous for my name, number, time of service, &c. It was not long before the sister in

A friendly Boer family watching a British ambulance waggon, full of sick & wounded, going into Pretoria.

charge of our ward appeared; she is Irish (Sister Strohan), and naturally very kind. Our tent holds six men, and we were all new arrivals that evening. She asked if we had had anything to eat, and we said we had had nothing beyond a little porridge at four in the morning. Then she commanded the orderlies to get "these *poor* men" bread, marmalade, cocoa, beef tea, pillows and all sorts of things. And we "poor men" laid comfortably in our beds and grinned at one another. She ordered us later to go to sleep, but we could not. For myself, I had not been in a bed for so long that I positively felt restless, and almost rolled out of bed so as to have a comfortable "doss" on the ground (it seemed like a case of the pig returning to its wallowing). At last I fell asleep, and once in that state took a good deal of arousing—for night nurses and orderlies tread more lightly than stable guards, and loose horses grazing round one's head.

Thursday, December 20th. A friend, of the Fife Yeomanry, came in here wounded last night. He went up with twenty other men of his crowd to reinforce the Northumberlands on the hill. Out of these, six were killed and nine wounded. I have already told you many of the dead and wounded were left on the kopjes for several days. He tells me it was horrible to see some of the poor fellows; the flies had got on their wounds. One fellow with a wounded jaw had maggots inside as well as out, and they were taken out of his mouth with little bits of stick. Another with a wounded side was quite a heaving, moving mass of them where he had been hit.

Christmas in Hospital.

IMPERIAL YEOMANRY HOSPITAL,
PRETORIA.
Monday, December 24th, 1900.

Here's to the doc's an' the nusses,
The bloomin' ord'lies too,
Who tend to us poor worn cusses,
All of 'em good and true.
Fightin' with death unceasin',
With ne'er a word of brag,
Sorrow an' anguish easin',
Under the Red Cross flag.
Extract from forthcoming "Orspital Odes."

Christmas Eve! Forsooth! And it falls on a homesick British Army in South Africa, home-yearning and longing for a sight of the sea (our sea!) like the famous Grecian host of old. If you ask a British soldier, "How goes it?" he promptly growls, "Feddup." I wonder what the Grecian warrior's equivalent for "fed up" was. He had one I am sure.

Christmas Eve, forsooth! Where is the prickly, red-berried holly? Where, too, the mistletoe with its pearly berries? And where, most of all, queries your enforced member of a Blue Ribbon Army—where is the Wassail Bowl?

The weather is fine, and under our tents we don't feel the heat of the sun. After the monotony of khaki here, there and everywhere, to which one gets accustomed on the veldt, the colours one sees here are quite enlivening. To begin with, *place aux dames* the nurses are arrayed in grey, white and red, and the patients who arrive in torn, worn, dirty or bloody khaki, surrender all their warlike habiliments to an orderly, have a bath and then "blossom in purple and red"—pyjamas, or in pinks, stripes or spots.

The food is very good here, and, as Tommy says, there is *bags* of it. "Bags" is the great Army word for abundance. It is used apparently without discrimination, and so one hears of bags of jam, bags of beer, bags of bags, bags of fun, or anything else in or out of reason.

For a student of dialect this hospital opens a large field. It is a regular Babel at times, our Sister speaking a superior Irish and the orderly an inferior brogue. In our tent are a Scotch, two Welsh, a Dorset and a Sussex Yeoman. In the next tent are some regulars of the Northumberland Fusiliers and Yorkshire Light Infantry, and a true-bred cockney Hussar, and their speech requires careful attention if the listener wishes to understand it, I can assure you. A few Kaffirs talking a bastard Dutch and an old Harrovian, who stutters like an excited soda water syphon, completes the Babel in my immediate neighbourhood.

The Irish orderly, Mick, by the way, is one of the most wonderful and plausible fellows I have met out here. To say he could talk a donkey's hind leg off would be a mild way of describing his excessive volubility—he would chatter a centipede's legs off. Often when he comes in, with another orderly's broom, to make a pretence of sweeping the tent

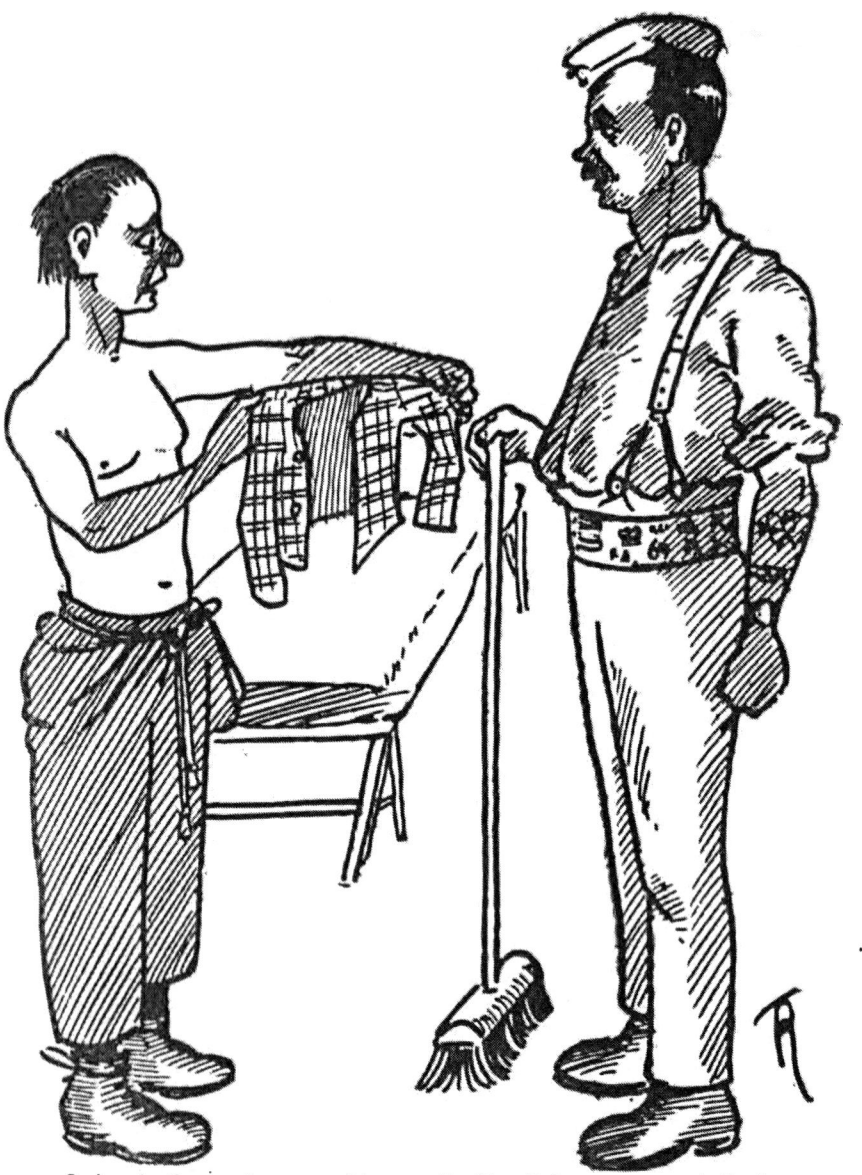

Owing to the great wear and tear on the Hospital garments and the large influx of fresh patients—pyjama suits are very rare in a perfect state or satisfactory size. Slippers also are excessively scarce. The above is a common scene.

ORDERLY (to complaining new patient): "*Well, it's the best Oi can do for yez.*"

out, and leaning on the stick, starts retailing stories of mystery and imagination, I lay down the book I am trying to read, and closing my eyes, drift into the land of true romance.

It is a land uninhabited by ladyes fayre in the general way, for the *dramatis personæ* usually comprise "th' ortherly corp'ril"; "th' sargint of th' gyard"; " th' qua'thermasther, an' a low blaygyard he waz"; "th' gin'ril o' th' disthrict"; "a lif'tint in 'H' Company"; and other military personages, with "th' ortherly room" or a "disthrict coort-martial" thrown in. If I had only had a phonograph I would preserve them, and when I get home, have them set up in type, tastily bound, and announced as "Tales from the Ill, by R—. K—.," and then live a life of opulent ease on the proceeds thereof.

"Th' sisther," as he calls her, says he is a dreadful man, and from her point of view I don't think she is far away from the truth. He argues about everything, and is always blaming his fellow orderlies. Still, it is the dreadful men who are invariably so entertaining.

I have just heard that a friend, Trooper Bewes, a cheery fellow of the Devons, has succumbed to his wound. Christmas Eve, forsooth! His chum was shot through the stomach, and died on the veldt. Poor fellow, he (the chum) was always swallowing with avidity any rumour about our going home—perhaps he was too keen, and ironical fate stepped in. It's a hard Christmas Box for his poor people, is it not?

We are debating whether to hang our socks up or not. If I do, and get something inside, it will probably be a scorpion. I found one in my boot a few days ago. The latest from our cheerful town pessimist, is "Don't be surprised if you are out another twelve months." Our Harrovian friend has summed up our feelings very aptly by stuttering, "If I had a bigger handkerchief I'd weep."

A couple of orderlies have just passed our tent, bearing an inanimate blanket-covered form on a stretcher—the last of my poor Devon friend, beyond a doubt. Another was carried by about two hours ago, while we were having tea. Christmas Eve, forsooth! Well, I will resume this tomorrow, or on Boxing Day.

Christmas Day.

There are not many people who would do any letter-writing on the afternoon of this day. But out here one does marvellous deeds, which one would never dream of attempting at home. So here I am, my dinner finished, adding a few lines to this letter, commenced yesterday.

Last night, in lieu of the festive carol singers, our waits (pickets) entertained us nearly all the night with volleys and independent firing. Whether the foe was real or imaginary I have not yet heard, but I believe the former. At four this morning I was awakened to have a fomentation on my leg, and drowsily realised it was Christmas Day. Then I fell asleep again, and dreamed of horrible adventures with Brother Boer. When we all awakened, we tried hard to convince one another it was indeed Christmas Day; one man actually going to the length of looking in his sock with a sneer, and all through the day "this time last year" anecdotes have been going strong amongst us of the I.Y.

"And a sorrow's crown of sorrows
Is remembering happier things."

After breakfast I strolled up to the post-office tent on a forlorn hope for letters. There were none for me, but one and a fine Scotch shortbread for the wounded Fife man in the bed next to mine. The cake, the beauty of which we quickly marred, was tastefully decorated with sugared devices, and the inscription, "Ye'll a' be welcome hame!"

Another fomentation, a visit from the doctor, who put us all on stout, and dinner was up. This consisted of the roast beef of Old—oh, no, it didn't, it was roast old trek ox, and I was unable to damage it with my well-worn teeth, so left it. The "duff" was not bad, and the quantity being augmented by a cold tinned one, which our Harrovian friend produced from his haversack, we fared very well, finishing up the repast with shortbread and a small bottle of stout each, with a diminutive pineapple for dessert.

Everybody I meet seems agreed on one point, and that is there has been no Christmas this year. Well, let us hope we shall have a real old-fashioned one next year.

New Year's Eve.

"The year is dying, *let him die*."

Them's my sentiments—"let him die." Despite the *nil nisi bonum* sentiment, I can't find it in my heart to say (at this present time and in my present humour) a good word for the dying year, his last days having been ones to be remembered with—er—oblivion only, so to speak. Since writing last, I have been flying high—that is to say, my temperature has—having registered 104·4 (don't omit the point) for a couple of days. I was rather proud of this, for, as you know, I didn't swagger in here with a fever or anything like that. No, I simply and quietly waited about a week, and then let them see what I could do without any real effort. And that is the right way to do things.

Look at Kitchener. People out here have been saying: "Wait till Kitchener is in command," and "Kitchener will do this and that." I sincerely hope he will. Mick, our day orderly, has just told me that "to hear people spake, ye'd think he cud brake eggs wid a hard stick,"—which I believe is his sarcastic way of summing up hero worship. I suggested most men could do that; whereupon Mick retorted: "Ye don't know, they might miss 'em." You never catch Mick napping. I only wish I could record the story of how he chucked the kits of "the Hon. Goschen and a nephew of the Juke of Portland's" out of one of the tents in 22 Ward, because they didn't choose the things which they wanted kept out, and let him take the rest away to the store tent. Needless to say, he was unaware at the time that he was entertaining angels.

Kitchener visited the Hospital some time ago but I missed seeing him. I was sleeping at the time, and was awakened by his voice inquiring how we were, and turned round just in time to see a khaki mackintosh disappear through the door. Of course, I had met him before. He turned me out of a house at which the C.-in-C. and staff had luncheon the day we were marching on Johannesburg. My luncheon on that occasion consisted of a nibble at a small, raw potato.

148 A YEOMAN'S LETTERS.

Sick.

"Who said 'C.I.V.'s'?"

(With apologies to the talented painter of "Who said 'Rats'!")

PARODY 9800134.
(Only one verse.)
When you've said "the war is over," and "the end is now in sight,"
  And you've welcomed home your valiant C.I.V.'s,
There are other absent beggars in the everlasting fight,
  And not the least of these your Yeoman, please.
He's a casual sort of Johnnie, and his casualties are great,
  And on the veldt and kopjes you will find him,
For he's still on active service, eating things without a plate,
  And thinking of the things he's left behind him.

I'll spare you the chorus.

The accompanying sketch, perhaps, needs a little explanation. To be brief, the British Army feels aggrieved at the praise bestowed on the C.I.V. Regiment, and its early return to England. To hear a discussion on our poor unoffending and former comrades is to have a sad exhibition of envy, hatred, malice, and all uncharitableness.

Any amount of fellows have got bad teeth, and when one considers the trek-ox and the army biscuit, one cannot be surprised. A lance-corporal of ours went before the doctor last week on this score; he had practically no teeth, and has been *sent into Pretoria on a month's furlough.* It is generally circulated in the squadron that the authorities expect fresh ones to grow in that time.

Tuesday, January 1st, 1901.

I saw the New Year in—in bed. There is little or no news, when we do get some it is usually unsatisfactory. I suppose you know we have no paper in Pretoria; the best they can do for us is to let us buy for a tikkie the *Bloemfontein Post*, always four days old, and its contents! The same brief, ancient and censored war news, the inspired leading article, a column on a cricket match between two scratch Bloemfontein teams, a treason trial, advertisements for I.L.H. and other recruits, and that is about all. Well, here's "A Happy New Year to us all."

There are some terrible dunder-headed beings in this world of ours. I saw one the day I came through Pretoria to this hospital. We were acquaintances in London, and with the eye of a hawk he picked me out of a load of dirty, khaki-clad wretches, and pounced on me with "What on earth did you come out here for?" I told him "to play knuckle bones."

In the tent next to this is a quiet man with a gun-shot wound in his knee. He is Vicary, V.C., of the Dorset Regiment. You may remember he won it in the Tirah campaign for a deed immeasurably superior to that of Findlater's; he saved an officer's life by killing five Afridis, shooting two and bayoneting and butt-ending the rest—a messy job. He is a small, quiet man, and wild horses could not induce him to talk of the winning of his V.C. He won't say a "blooming" word on the subject to anyone, not even an orderly.

We have a small library in the hospital (Mrs. Dick Chamberlain's). I got Max O'Rell's "John Bull and Co." from it a few days ago. It concludes with the author's reply to a question asked him the day before he left South Africa.

"Well, after all these long travels what are you going to do now?"

"What am I going to do?" he replied; "I am going to Europe to look at an old wall with a bit of ivy on it."

And, by the Lord Harry, that's just what I want to do myself.

* * * *

I'm getting rather tired of my prolonged loaf in Arcadia, for that is the name of this part of Pretoria, and although it is really not my fault, still I feel ashamed of myself for not being with the company.' Still, even if I were out of the hospital, I should merely be able to join a number of details of Sussex, Devon, Dorset, Fife, and other Yeomen who are waiting in Pretoria an indefinite time for remounts and fresh equipment. I daresay my last letter, if it arrived at all arrived later than usual, as the day the mails left here there was a biggish fight a few miles down the line at the first station (Irene), and the train had to return. It is also rumoured that the home mails due were held up and collared, a hardy perennial this.

All last Friday we could hear big guns pounding away, and we heard on Saturday that the enemy had pulled up a good deal of the line, but the fort, or forts, at Irene had held their own. In addition to this, rumour hath it that Delarey and eight hundred (or 500, or 1,000) have been killed or captured, also that Clements has been killed. But all this, as usual, needs confirmation. So inaccurate or vague is actual news when we do get it, that a big fight might take place in the nearest back-garden, and we should be absolutely ignorant of the real details of the combat.

I have just heard that the news that General Clements is dead is correct. He died of a wound received some days ago I am told. If it is true, we have lost another good officer and brave man.

We certainly have made every use of our privilege as Englishmen to grumble since we have been out here. A certain Bill Fletcher, erstwhile a Cockney pot boy, now of Kitchener's Horse, has just taken a bed in our tent, and has announced that he is tired of the "blooming" country, where the "blooming" flowers don't smell, the "blooming" birds don't sing, and the "blooming" fruit don't taste (this latter charge is not quite correct), and he wants to get back to the "blooming" fog and smoke of London; all this, and he has only been at it five months.

The Career of an Untruth.

Clements is not dead, and Delarey and his friends are not captured.

I am telling you the latest rumours and anti-rumours, as this letter progresses.

And yet the man I had the first version from had had it from an R.A.M.C. Sergeant, who had it on the most reliable authority of the commandant's orderly, who had heard the commandant tell it to the P.M.O. He had also been corroborated by a man who had seen the man who took it down from the heliograph. Also one of the hospital runners had heard Dr. —— tell Dr. ——, and a friend of his had a friend who knew a man on the officers' mess, who had seen it up in orders, distinctly.

A Tommy came in just now and said "Hullo, Corporal!" I shook his flipper weakly and tried the dodge of pretending to recognise him. But I had to give it up, and admit I could not for the moment recognise him, and thought he had made a mistake. To which he replied he had not, and didn't I remember the soap. I did.

About two months or more ago, having halted at midday at some fontein or other *en route* for Rustenburg, Whiteing and I went down to the nearest stream to have the usual wash. There we found heaps of fellows washing; but, alas! there was a great dearth of soap. A Northumberland man asked me if I could sell him some, and I gave him a small chunk. The demand was great, and there was practically no supply, When we got back to our lines, Whiteing, ever forgetful, discovered he had left his precious brown Windsor behind. It was too late to go back to try and find it, so he gave up all hopes of ever seeing it again. The next day, as we were riding through the infantry advance guard of the Border Regiment, one of the fellows shouted to me, asking if I had lost any soap the day before. I replied "No," and then recollected Whiteing's loss added that a friend of mine had. My infantry friend thereupon promised to bring it round in the evening, which he did. In this manner we became acquainted with him. I mention this incident just to show what a really good sportsman the true Thomas is. Here was soap in great request: we were strangers to him, having merely chatted with him and the others as we washed in the mud and water, and yet, without our even making enquiries for the precious lump, he went out of his way to return it.

I asked him why he had come into the hospital, and he told me he and several others had been sent in as unfit for the veldt, and so were to act as hospital orderlies. When I inquired how he liked the idea, he said it was all right, as he was clear of the horrible "hundred-and-fifty," and he laid his hands significantly where the pouches are wont to decorate the waist of the poor infantryman.

[*Note.*—I suppose you know the infantryman's cross is the hated 150 rounds in the two pouches, which after many miles marching become most irksome, especially for the muscles of the stomach.]

I, of course, inquired after Nobby, but he could not tell me anything about him, as Nobby is in "H" Company and his was "B."

To-day (the 16th) a large number of fellows are leaving here for the base and, the rumour is—*home*.

Got his ticket.
"See that fellow?"
"Yes."
"He's 'marked for home'."
Lucky Beggar!

The P.M.O. asked a Yeomanry friend yesterday if he would like to go home or join his squadron, and the Yeoman's reply was he would like to rejoin his squadron— at home. In explanation, he smilingly stated that all of his squadron's officers, bar one, had gone home, and nearly all the squadron, having been invalided or discharged. Well, I think this is long enough for a letter written by a man who can hardly claim to be "on active service" just at present.

The Sisters' Albums.

Sunday, January 26th, 1901.

Still at the above address, but going strong, and almost losing the Spartan habits engendered by my recent life on the veldt!

News is very scarce with us, and to dare to write you a long letter would be the height of impudence, so I will let you off with a moderately short one this week.

Last week an original burlesque (perhaps I ought to politely designate it a musical comedy) was produced in a large marquee here, which is called "the theatre." I don't know what the name of the piece was but it dealt with a Hospital Commission, and the *dramatis personæ* consisted of a Boer spy, posing as the Commissioner, the real Commissioner, as a new nurse, nurses, orderlies, Kaffirs and doctors, amongst the latter being a Scotch Doctor, who drank a deal of "whuskey" and whose diagnoses were most entertaining. It was quite pathetic to watch the keen interest with which the audience followed the diversions of "Dr. Sandy" with the bottle.

I have been concerned in "doing something" in our day nurse's album lately (I think I have already alluded to the presence of the album evil out here). I have willingly volunteered to contribute to these volumes, hoping to see their contents, but, alas, in most cases I have had to start the tome; however, in the present case the album has been well started by various patients. Most of the efforts are strikingly original and all in verse, so I determined to do something for the honour of the county of my birth, and, securing a pen and ink, perpetrated some Michael Angelic-like sketches of "the-ministering-angel-thou," order. Then,

hearing that a poem (scratch a Tommy and you'll find a poet) was expected, valiantly started off with something like this:
"She wore a cape of scarlet,
The eve when first we met;
A gown of grey was on her form
(I wore some flannelette!):
She was a sister to us all,
And yet no relation;
She stuck upon my dexter leg,
A hot fomentation."

But appearing suggestive of something else, I crossed it out and finally produced the following ambitious ode:—

THE GREAT PANACEA.

Poets from time of yore have sung
In every clime and every tongue,
Of beauty and the pow'r of love,
Of things on earth and things above.

Sonnets to ladyes' eyes indited,
And for such stuff been killed or knighted.
They've raved on this and raved on that,
The dog or the domestic cat.

On blessëd peace and glorious war,
On deeds of daring dashed with gore,
And scores of other wondrous deeds,
Which History or Tradition heeds.

But I would humbly sing to praise
Something unhonoured in those lays—
The cure for broken legs and arms,
For suff'rers of rheumatic qualms.

For wounds by bullet or the knife,
Obtained in peace or deadly strife;
For broken heads or spraineïd toes,
And myriad other sorts of woes,
For that incurable disease
"Fed up" or "tired of C.I.V.'s,"

For pom-pom fever, Mauseritis,
The toothache or the loafertitis.
For broken heart or broken nose,
For every sickness science knows.

All these and ev'ry other ill,
Are cured by that well-known Pill;
'Tis made on earth with pow'rs divine,
I sing in praise of *Number Nine*.

To expatiate further upon the famous "No. 9 Pill" would be absurd, as it is as great an institution of the British Army out here as the 4.7 or pom-pom.

156 A YEOMAN'S LETTERS.

We are still suffering (worse than ever) from a paucity of news and a superabundance of rumours; indeed the supply of the latter far exceeds the demand, and budding fictionists eclipse themselves daily. Had the Psalmist lived

Thoughtless Sister (persuasively): "Now I want you to do something very nice in my Album."

in these days, I feel sure he would hardly have contented himself with the gentle statement that "all men are liars," but have indulged in language far more emphatic. Still as far as we are concerned, the Boers can beat the most brilliant efforts of our own fellows any day.

We have a lot of Regulars in this hospital, and it is amusing at times, and at others rather irritating, to hear some of their criticisms of the Yeomanry. I recently heard some of them (good fellows) chaffing merrily over certain Yeomanry (a very small number), who were concerned in an unfortunate affair some time ago, totally ignoring the fact that a *large* number of Regular Infantry and Mounted Infantry were also equally involved. Again the Cavalry may make a mistake, and they have made a few, but we don't hear much about their incapacity, but let the Yeomanry commit a similar error, and we hear about it, I can tell you. I venture these few remarks in common fairness to the Yeomanry, my temperature being quite normal, as I fancy they have often been used as a butt where others would have done as well.

The explanation, it appears, is this. A corps of new Yeomanry is being formed, who are to receive five shillings a day; we also, of the original Yeomanry, are to receive the same at the expiration of a year's service, having up till then been paid the regular cavalry pay, for which we enlisted. Naturally, Thomas A. feels exceedingly wroth at "blooming ammychewers" receiving such remuneration, and to use his own metaphor, "chews the fat" accordingly. His position and feelings remind me very strongly of the poor soldier in "The Tin Gee-Gee!"

>Then that little tin soldier he sobbed and sighed,
> So I patted his little tin head,
>"What vexes your little tin soul?" said I,
> And this is what he said:
>"I've been on this stall a very long time,
> And I'm marked '1/3' as you see,
>While just above my head he's marked '5 bob,'
> Is a bloke in the Yeoman-ree.
>Now he hasn't any service and he hasn't got no drill,
> And I'm better far than he,
>Then why mark us at fifteen pence,
> And five bob the Yeoman-ree?"
>   etc.   etc.   etc.

I am very sorry for poor friend Thomas.

On Wednesday (the 23rd) we heard the sad news that our Queen was dead. It came as quite a blow to us, and even now seems hardly credible; we had only heard the previous day of her serious condition. All through the Hospital everyone seems to be experiencing a personal bereavement. I overheard a Tommy remark, in a subdued tone full of respect, when he was told the news, "Well she done her jewty." And I am sure it summed up his and our feelings very accurately. A man has also told me of the death of Captain McLean, at Krugersdorp, which is very sad; he always looked so fit. Mr. Cory is now captain of our squadron and the only Sussex Yeomanry officer in South Africa.

"Long live the King!"

January 30th, 1901.

You will soon begin to think that I am a permanent boarder at this place; indeed, I almost feel so myself now; though as a matter of fact I am expecting to be marked out any hour—the sooner the better, for the enforced inactivity is by no means free from monotony, not to mention headaches, toothaches, and sleepless nights, from which one seldom suffers on the veldt. I have found out a dodge for obtaining a better night's sleep than is one's usual lot, and that is a good pitched pillow fight before turning in. Of course, it is advisable not to be caught by the night sister.

Last night we had a terrific storm, and had to stand by the poles and tent walls for a long time. The wind, hail and rain were tremendous, and in spite of our tents all being on sloping ground, with trenches a foot deep around them, we got a bit of moisture in as it was.

On Monday, His Majesty King Edward VII., was proclaimed in Pretoria, a salute of guns fired from the Artillery barracks, and all flags temporarily mast-headed, and back to you good folks at home we sent echoing our loyal sentiment, "God save the King."

On Saturday, Whiteing waltzed gaily up and paid me a visit, having got leave into Pretoria from Rietfontein, where he had been left with other men, all minus noble quadrupeds, and on Sunday another old comrade, the Great Boleno, darkened the door of our tent and brightened me with the

light of his presence. He had been one of Clements'
orderlies for the last two months, and had accompanied the
general into Pretoria, and succeeded in securing a good
civil berth in the town.

"God save the King!"
January 1901.

From these I learnt the fortunes of the battalion up to
date. Briefly, after I left them they were some time at
Rietfontein; then at Buffalspoort, where they did delightful
guards, pickets, and early morning standing to horses; after
which those possessed of horses went on to Rustenburg,

I believe, where they now are, the horseless ones going back into Rietfontein.

So now the Seventh Battalion of Imperial Yeomanry, like many others, is spread well over the face of the land.* Some of the fellows are home; some on their way thither; some in this hospital, some in others; some are in the police; some in civil employment; some with sick horses at Rietfontein; some in a detail camp at Elandsfontein (near Johannesburg); some with the battalion, at Rustenburg; and some, alas, are not.

Whiteing gave me a vivid description of his journey into Pretoria on one of the steam-sappers running between that town and Rietfontein; they are known as the Pretoria-Rietfontein expresses. As he put it, they stop for nothing, over rocks, through spruits and dongas, squelch over one of French's milestones here and there, the ponderous iron horse snorted on its wild career till its destination was reached.

The Irish Fusilier's Ambition.

Though I am well off for literature of all sorts (my locker is a scandal), I don't seem to be able to settle down to anything like a quiet, enjoyable read at all. Tommy Atkins *never* seems to realise that one cannot carry on a conversation and read a book simultaneously, or write a letter.

"Oh for a booke and a shadie nooke,
  Eyther indoore or out;
With the grene leaves whysperynge overheade,
  Or the streete cryes all about.
Where I maie reade all at mine ease,
  Both of the newe and olde;
For a jollie goode booke whereon to looke,
  Is better to me than golde."

Thus the olde songe. And the kopjes are gazing stonily at me through the tent door; a man two beds off is squirming and ejaculating under the massage treatment of a powerful khaki *masseur;* doctors, sisters, orderlies, and runners come and go; a triangular duel between three patients on the usual subject—the superior merits of their respective regiments—is in full swing; and the realisation of the foregoing rhyme seems afar off.

* The subsequent adventures of the battalion under General Cunningham and later Dixon and Benson I am, of course, unable to record.

I, however, am not the only man with yearnings for a different state of affairs. Private Patrick McLaughlan, of the Inniskilling Fusiliers, occupying the bed on my right, has his. He often tells us his ideal of happiness, a "pub" corner with half-a-dozen pint pots containing ambrosial "four 'arf" before him, and a well-seasoned old clay three inches long filled with black Irish twist.

The other day I ventured to Omarise his ideal of the earthly paradise thus:

> A pipe of blackish hue for smoking fit,
> Some good ould Irish twist to put in it;
> Six pints of beer in a hostel snug,
> And there, a king in Paradise, I'd sit.

His only comment was a vast expectoration.

By-the-way, my friend, Patrick, relates a good loot tale which befell his regiment in the Free State. They camped one day within easy distance of a store, kept by the usual gentleman of Hebrew extraction. Pat and his comrades made a rush for the place and collared all of the condensed milk, for which the merchant charged (or attempted to) a shilling per tin. About five men, early arrivals, paid; then in the scramble which ensued the rest omitted to do likewise. On returning to camp and opening the tins the milk appeared peculiar, and the regimental Æsculapius hearing of it, inspected the tins, pronounced them bad, and told the men to take them back to the store and get *their money* refunded, which they did. Of course, the gentle Hebrew protested vehemently, but Tommy, with the medical officer's word behind him, soon persuaded him to do what he was told. Patrick was six shillings to the good over this transaction. And I daresay the wily Israelite regretted having had such a large stock of milk, though presumably he had hoped to rob the Philistines, not, as the case proved, to be doubly done by them.

"War without End."

(An Interlude.)

He came up to me and handed me a photograph. I took it, and beheld a being clad in a new khaki uniform and obviously conscious of the fact. An empty bandolier crossed his extended chest diagonally. His slouch hat was well tilted to the right, with the chin strap arranged just under the lower lip. The putties were immaculately entwined around his legs—in short the *tout ensemble* was decidedly smart and soldier-like. His right hand rested lightly on a Sheraton table; in the immediate background was a portion of a low ornamental garden wall, in the distance was a ruin principally composed of Ionic columns in various positions—presumably the devastating work of the warrior in the foreground, "Look on that," he said bitterly, and as I returned it, "and on this, the *backbone* of the British Army," smiting his manly breast. I looked, and in the bronzed, unshaven face and raggedly-apparelled figure before me, recognised a certain semblance to him of the photograph. I smiled sympathetically. "As it was," quoth he, "now and ever shall be, war without end." I turned to go, but was not fated to escape so easily. He held me with his bloodshot eyes, and perforce I stayed. With upraised voice he declaimed thus:

THE PSALM OF STRIFE.
(*Being what the Yeoman said to the Psalmist.*)

Tell me not in ceaseless rumours
That we soon are going home,
Just to cure our bitter humours,
While upon the veldt we roam.

War is real, and war is earnest,
And Pretoria warn't the goal,
Out thou cam'st, but when returnest
Is not known to any soul.

Forward, fighting, smoking, chewing,
With a heart for any fate,
Still achieving, still pursuing,
And arriving—*just too late*.

I fled.

Invitations—and a Concert.

Wednesday, February 6th, 1901.

Another week has rolled away; a week's march nearer home anyway, and like the great MacMahon, I am here and here I sticks. The most thrilling event of the past seven days has been the sudden and unexpected reception of mails, after having abandoned all hope, and a parcel which arrived in Pretoria for me during the first week in September.

I was interested to read in an enclosed note that my aunt hoped I should be home to spend Christmas with her. By-the-bye, people have been awfully good in sending me invitations to weddings, funerals, and christenings. In August last I was the recipient of a dainty invitation to the wedding of a friend. The sad event was to take place in June. I didn't go. The latest was a cream-laid affair, from another quarter, on which I was requested in letters of gold to honour certain near and dear relatives with my presence at the christening of their first-born. As the affair was to take place in December, and I received the pressing invitation at the end of January—I was again unable to be present at another interesting ceremony. I have also received several invitations to Terpsichorean revels. My R.S.V.P. has been curtly to the effect that "Mr. P. T. R. is not dancing this season."

As regards deaths and funerals, I have seen and attended more than enough of them out here. At this present moment a friend, a New Zealander, is in parlous plight. He was shot in the right shoulder, the wound soon healed, but the arm was almost useless, so the massage fiend here used to come and give him terrible gip. Then doctor No. 3 came along, said he had been treated wrongly, that the artery was severed, etc., and operated on him. The operation itself was successful, but as regards other matters, it is touch and go with him, his arm is black up to a little above the elbow, in places it is ebony, and, I understand, amputation, if the worse comes to the worst, is almost out of the question. So, with others, I go in to keep him cheered up, and chaff him over the champagne and other luxuries he is on, suggesting what a lovely black eye his ebony right mawler might give a fellow, and feeling all the time a strong inclination to do a sob. He is such a rattling fine fellow, indeed, all the Colonials I have met are.*

---

* Since my return I have heard from "Scotty," as we used to call him. He wrote from his home in New Zealand, his right arm had been successfully amputated, and he was getting accustomed to its loss.

Last night we had an open-air concert; the best part of it, as is often the case at such affairs, appeared to be the refreshments which were provided for the officers and artists. The talent was really not of a high order, being supplied from Pretoria.

The chairman, who introduced the performers and announced the items, affording us most entertainment, usually, unconsciously, he being a long-winded individual, and invariably commencing his remarks with "Er-hem! Ladies and gentleman, a great Greek philosopher once said "—or "There is an old proverb." He essayed to give us "The dear Homeland," but being interrupted in one of his most ambitious vocal flights by a giddy young officer (and a gentleman) throwing a bundle of music and a bunch of vegetables at him, hastily finished his song, and in a dignified voice requested us to conclude the proceedings by singing "God Save the Quing." This was the first time I had sung the National Anthem, since the death of our Queen, and I felt, as no doubt everybody has experienced, a most peculiar feeling on singing the words, "God Save the King."

Then to bed, but not to sleep, for that is a difficult matter here—so I laid and chatted with a trooper of Roberts' Horse, the latest occupant of the next bed to me. He is, or rather was, a schoolmaster, wears spectacles and is grey-headed; what induced him to join in this little game heaven, and he, only know. In the midst of a discussion on the Afrikander Bond and the South African League, the night sister came in and imperiously bade us be silent and go to sleep. So the grey-headed schoolmaster and my humble self, like guilty children, became silent, and serenaded by the ubiquitous mosquito wooed sweet Morpheus.

Thursday, February 7th. Last night it rained steadily nearly all night; and it has just recommenced. It is quite an agreeable change to see a leaden sky and hear the rain softly pattering on the tent roof, after many days of sweltering, dazzling heat, *when one is in a comfortable tent.* But it makes me think of and wish for a comfortable room at home, a good book, pipe, and an easy chair, the prospect outside beautifully dreary and rainy, a fire in front of me and my slippered feet on the library mantelpiece.

A rather amusing incident occurred just now. One of the Devon Yeomanry who went up to the tent which is our post-office, on the off-chance of getting a letter, to his great astonishment got one. He came back eyeing the address suspiciously, and remarking, "It's tracts, I'm thinkin.'" His conjecture turned out correct. It appears that a certain thoughtful and religious society at home looks down the lists of the wounded and, now and again, sends some of the worst cases tracts. The title of one of the pamphlets was, "I've got my ticket," which amused us immensely, for to get one's ticket means to be booked for home. Another title was "The finger of God"—this to a man who has had an explosive bullet through his forearm seems rather rough.

I fear my letters are becoming dreadfully reminiscent and anecdotal, but adventures and wanderings are not for the man who loafs in hospital.

Wednesday, February 13th. I am all *kiff* (military for "right"). This morning we had a mild joke with a new night orderly. As you may be aware, it is this gentleman's duty to wash all the bad bed patients. When he came in soon after *reveillé* and asked if there were any bed patients to be washed, we all feebly replied, "Yes, all of us," and he had ablutionised three before he discovered the deception, when he anathematised us all.

News is more rigorously suppressed than ever, and undoubtedly it is the right thing to do. Everybody is of this opinion, for the *friendly* Dutch in Pretoria and elsewhere used to know far too much.

Our Orderly's Blighted Heart.

Friday. Yesterday was unfortunately the day of Valentine the Saint. I say "unfortunately" for this reason: I was just about to continue this letter, when our day orderly came in, and taking advantage of my sympathetic and credulous nature, after boldly reminding me that it was St. Valentine's Day, told me that he had only loved once and never would again.

In this respect he differs considerably from the majority of orderlies. He then comfortably arranged himself on a vacant bed, and unsolicited, with a smiling face, told me the romantic story of his blighted affection. As it may interest you, I will give you a condensed version of the same. Would to Heaven he had so dealt with me. But I was born to suffer, and was I not in hospital? As a coster lad he went with a young woman who loved him. He also loved her. Her name was Olivia. She went upon the "styge," and loved him still. Then an old nobleman (Sir ——) fell in love with her, followed her persistently, and wooed her through her parents. He was rich but honest, and it was a case of December and April, for she was all showers—of tears. At last, against her heart's dictates, she married him and became an old man's pet—nuisance, I should imagine, and my orderly friend became a soldier. Alas for the trio, she could not forget her old, I mean young, love, and eventually blew her brains out in Paris. They spattered the ceiling and ruined the carpet—I forgot the rest, (there was a lovely account of it in the *People*), for over-taxed nature could stand no more, and I fell asleep dreaming of reporters wading ankle-deep in blood in a Louis Quatorze drawing-room, taking notes of a terrible tragedy in high life, and was horrified to hear a loud report, followed by a gurgling sound, and, opening my eyes, beheld—Mr. Orderly holding one of my bottles of stout upside down to his lips, and in his other hand my corkscrew with a cork on the end of it.

Private McLaughlan, of the Inniskillings, having heard of this, informed me that he "jined th' Army" because his father would not let him keep five racehorses; and Private Hewitt, of the 12th M.I., gave his reason as being his refusal to marry a *h*eiress. After this our orderly ceased from troubling—for a time.

Amongst the many sad cases I have come across, here is one which strikes me as being particularly pitiable. A poor fellow of the 2nd Lincolns is the patient I am thinking about. He is deaf, deaf as a stone wall, is sickening for enteric, cannot read, and is at times delirious. The tent the poor fellow is in is not a very good one, and he seems quite friendless. There he lies in his bed, never uttering a word or hearing one, and as helpless as a child. Some mornings back I saw him eating his porridge with his fingers, the man who had handed it to him having forgotten to give him a spoon. His utter loneliness seems too awful. I wonder what his poor mind thinks about. When told that he would probably be sent home, he said he did not want to go. Surely somewhere in God's sweet world there is somebody who cares for and thinks about him. I cannot half express to you the sadness of his solitude.

Southward Ho!

No. 2 Hospital Train,
Monday, February 18th.

On Friday I had my sheet marked with those magic words "For base," paraded on Saturday morning before the P.M.O., and a few hours later was told to go to the pack store, draw my kit, and be ready to entrain at five. So I had to rush about.

It was soon time to parade for the station, and I had to rush through as many leave-takings as possible. Good-bye to Sister Douglas, Sister Mavius, Sister O'Connor; to an Australian Bushman friend with injured toes, who hobbles about on his heels; to poor old Scotty, the New Zealander, as game as they make them, who is to have his right arm off on Monday (to-day); to a big, good-natured gunner of No. 10 Mountain Battery, whose acquaintance I had only just made; to a Piccadilly Yeoman; to our day orderly, and dozens of other good fellows, and I had said farewell, or perhaps only *au revoir*, to the I.Y. Hospital Arcadia, with the doctor of our ward, Dr. Douglas, one of the cleverest and best, the Sisters with their albums, and all its tragedies and comedies. Perjuring my soul beyond redemption by cordial promises to write to all and sundry, so I left them.

* * * *

Once aboard the lugger, I should say train, our berths were allotted to us, and we soon settled down. The whole thing is very much like being on shipboard, save that there the authorities are all for turning you out of your hammocks ("turn out o' them 'ammicks!"), and here they are all for keeping you in your bunk, the space being so limited. On each man's bed was a well-filled white canvas bag, being a present from the Good Hope and British Red Cross Societies. These were opened with no little curiosity. Strange to say one of the first things an old toothless Yorkshireman drew out was—a toothbrush. This caused general amusement. There was nothing shoddy about the contents of these bags; they contained a suit of pyjamas, shoes, a shirt, socks, towel, sponge bag with sponge, soap, and toothbrush in it, a hairbrush, and handkerchief. So could you but see me now, as I write, you would behold a being clad in a swagger suit of Cambridge blue pyjamas.

Before daybreak a terrific bang aroused us to the fact that the engine which was to bear us southward had come into action, and soon we were under way. At Elandsfontein we beheld the mail train *with our mails* going up. Farewell to mails! Kroonstad was reached at half-past two, and we were shunted into a siding till this morning, when we resumed our journey, passing *through* Bloemfontein, to our joy, and arriving at Springfontein soon after dark.

What a gigantic affair this war has been, and is. To travel through these countries, the Transvaal, Orange River Colony, and the Cape Colony (Tuesday morning, we are now in the latter) by rail alone is to feel all criticism silenced.

Already we have passed hundreds of miles of flat veldt, with now and again big kopjes in the background. At every station, bridge, and small culvert are bodies of regulars, militia, and volunteers, or colonial and other mounted troops. And when one considers that the bigger towns are being strongly held, also various posts all over these countries, and columns are operating in various districts, the whole affair fills one with wonder and admiration. We expect to reach Deelfontein this evening. An R.A.M.C. man has just been discussing that ghastly failure, inoculation, with another man. Said he: "Inoculation is bally tommy-rot!" Quoth the other, "That be hanged for a yarn. Tommy rot, indeed, it nearly killed me!" It's a fact, the unnecessary suffering which was endured by the poor beggars who allowed this experiment to be performed upon them, with the hope of spoofing the fever fiend, has been great. And strange to say, in many cases they (the inoculated) have been the first victims.

Once again we are amongst our old enemies, the kopjes, which, south of the Orange River Colony, begin to assert themselves again. There has been any amount of rain down this way, and muddy water is flowing like the milk and honey of the promised land. From wet tents and saturated blanket kennels bronzed ragamuffins appear at every halting spot, and simultaneously they and we ask each other the old, old question, "Any news?"

Sometimes they break the monotony of the negative by telling us that "De Wet is mortally wounded," or "has got away again," and we tell them that "Botha is surrounded." Some of the sanguine spirits aboard this train are buoying themselves up with the idea of getting home. Alas! there's many a slip 'twixt the land and the ship, as I fear they will find to their bitter disappointment.

It is now Tuesday evening. We have just reached Naauwpoort, where we are spending the night. The Cape mail train has been detained here all day, the line ahead having been blown up, or some such thing, a train derailed and fired on, a Yeoman and several niggers killed, and other fellows injured. Brother Boer seems more in evidence down here than in any other place we have passed between Pretoria and this place.

IMPERIAL YEOMANRY HOSPITAL,
DEELFONTEIN.

We arrived here on Thursday, February 21st. Between Naauwpoort and De Aar we passed the derailed train. Mr. Boer had done his work well — from his point of view. The engine (575) was lying on its side quite smashed, as were also several broken and splintered trucks, while a few graves completed the picture. But the line was intact once again. An officer of Engineers and some men were standing by their completed task as we slowly came up and passed the spot.

Line Clear: o'er blood and sweat, and pain, and sorrow's road I ran,
And every sleeper was a wound, and every rail a man.

The first person I beheld from the carriage window on arriving here was one of our Sussex fellows. He seemed very pleased to see me, and I certainly was to see him. He has been here a week or more, and in that time had acquainted himself with the ropes. Having been given accommodation in the emergency tent for the night, he took me by divers ways to a bell tent in which I found two or three men of Paget's Horse, acquaintances of the "Delphic" days, another Sussex man, and a large washing basin containing beer—obtained no matter how. Into the basin a broken cup and a tin mug were being constantly dipped. With this, cigarettes, and chatter, the evening passed very agreeably. Of course this is early to criticise the Hospital and its working, but the general impression of we ex-Arcadians is that the Pretoria shop is far superior.

As regards reaching Cape Town, one cannot say much. A good many of our fellows have been sent back to Elandsfontein, which has been styled as "the home for lost Yeomanry." In the station, a few hundred yards off, is a fine khaki armoured train, with a pom-pom named "Edward VII." mounted on the centre truck.

R.A.M.C. Experiences and Impressions.

WYNBERG HOSPITAL,
CAPE COLONY.
Monday, February 25th, 1901.

The above address may appear to you like a day's march nearer home, but it is more than likely nothing of the sort. Having once got the convalescent gentlemen in khaki down south as far as Cape Town, and raised the home yearning hearts of the aforementioned to an altitude beyond the loftiest peak of the Himalayas—the medical officers here return them as shuttlecocks from a battledore up country, and it's a case of "gentlemen in khaki ordered North."

We arrived here this morning early, having left Deelfontein at daybreak yesterday (Sunday). Ambulance carts conveyed us to the Wynberg Hospital, where I now am.

Tuesday, 26th. Wherever I go I seem to fall fairly well on my feet and meet old friends. In the next room (each ward is divided into rooms, these are barracks in time of peace) are two fellows who were in my tent at Pretoria; one was half-blinded by lightning. They are rattling good fellows. My bed chum, the man next to me, is a man of the Rifle Brigade, who has lost an eye, and, again, is a ripping fine chap. This is an R.A.M.C. show, and everything is regimental, dem'd regimental. We have

A YEOMAN'S LETTERS. 171

the regulation barrack-room cots, which have to be limbered up and dressed with the familiar brown blankets and sheets in apple-pie or, rather, Swiss roll, order. Also, the locker has to be kept very neat and symmetrical. To drop a piece of paper in the room would be almost courting a court-martial. So, whenever I have a small piece of paper

Tommy's Spittoon

In Hospital the bed-patients, whose principal pleasure in smoking seems to be the spitting, have recourse to the above.

to throw away, I roam about like a criminal anxious to conceal a corpse, and am often nearly driven to chewing and swallowing it, after the well-known method of famous heroes and criminals.

I have already referred to the confounded regimentality of this place. The very red cross on our virgin white R.A.M.C. banner is made of red tape, not bunting, I am positive. It almost goes without saying that we have to don, and never leave off, in the daytime, the cobalt blue uniform and huge red tie so dear to the controllers of these establishments. The blue trousers are terrible things, being lined with some thick material and kept up by a tape at the waist. A friend of mine in Paget's Horse will not have them called trousers, but always alludes to them as leg casings.

I am not quite so particular about my food as formerly, but the Imperial Yeomanry Hospital at Pretoria must have spoiled me. Then, again, there was the Deelfontein one, so I must set aside my own opinion and give you that of others. The food (in our ward) is little and poor; being one pound of bread and an ounce of butter per day for men on *full* rations, accompanied at morn and eventide by a purply fluid called "tea." At mid-day a tin of tough meat with a potato or two is served up, for which we are truly thankful. Amen! As regards recreation we get plenty of that—airing bedding, scrubbing lockers and floors, cleaning windows, whitewashing, washing our plates and other tinware after our sumptuous repasts, general tidying up, having rows with the sergeant-major, and a myriad other little pastimes help to while the hours away. In full view of our ward is the slate-coloured gun carriage which is used for conveying the unfittest to their last long rest. It is kept outside of a barn-like building, and its contemplation affords us much food (extra ration) for reflection. It is often used.

The Mythical and Real Officer.[*]

As I pause, and ponder what else I can tell you in this letter, it occurs to me that I have not yet told you of the one

---

[*] An officer, for whom I have the highest esteem, whilst kindly conveying to me his very favourable opinion of these "Letters," regretted the inclusion of the following "grouse" in these words: "When I think of many cheery, dirty, ragged, half-starved youngsters I met out there, weighted into an unaccustomed responsibility for men's lives and the safety of their columns, and no more their own masters than you were, bravely trying to do a duty which many of them really loathed, I feel it is hard that a minority of 'rotters' should blacken the good name of the majority."

great disillusion of this campaign for me and *all* other former civilians—I mean "The British Officer." The few remarks which I am now going to make are founded on the universal opinion of all the Regular soldiers and Colonial and home-bred Volunteers I have met out here. I have hesitated to give this verdict before, because it seemed like rank heresy or a kind of sacrilege; but having asked every man I have come across, especially the Regular soldier, his estimate of this person, and always receiving the same emphatic reply, I feel I can now make my few remarks without being regarded as too hasty or ill-informed.

There are officers who are real good fellows, and of these I will tell presently; but there are others—*heaps of others*. These latter are selfish, and frequently incompetent beings, without the slightest consideration for their men, and with a terrible amount for their dear selves. Talk about their roughing it! Most of these individuals have the best of camp beds to rest on, servants to wait on them, good stuff to eat, and, more often than not, whisky, or brandy to drink. And, oh, my sisters, oh, my brothers, when *they* have to commence roughing it, it is hard indeed for poor Tommy. Many a tale have I heard of thirsty tired Tommies being refused their water cart in camp, as the officers required the water out of it for their baths.

The beautiful stories, on the other hand, of the officer being troubled because his men were in bad case, and sharing the contents of his haversack or water bottle with a poor "done-up" Tommy, are generally pure fiction. To hear of Tommy sharing with a chum or a stranger is common enough. Out here one learns to appreciate the ranker more, and the commissioned man less. And when one comes across a good officer, how he is appreciated! Often when I have asked a regular what sort of officers he had, and received the invariable emphatic reply, he has stopped, and in quite a different voice, with a smile on his face, said, "But there was Mr. ———; now he was a *real* gentleman." And then he has waxed eloquent in this popular officer's praises, relating how "he used to be like one of ourselves," insisted on taking his relief at digging trenches, came and chatted to them round their fires at night, and in scores of ways endeared himself to their hearts.

My Rifle friend has just been telling me of such an officer, a young one they had, named Wilson (how he eulogised Mr. Wilson! "He was a good 'un, he was. A *real* gentleman"). He died, poor fellow, up Lydenburg way. Then he told me of another, a Mr. Baker-Carr; of him he said, "And there isn't a man of us to-day who, if he was in danger, wouldn't die for him."

As for the opinion of the Colonials of our officers, you surely know that. This little anecdote expresses pretty well how they stand one with the other:

SCENE—PRETORIA.

New Zealander, just in from trek, passing, pipe in mouth, by a young officer just out.

Officer (stopping New Zealander): "Do you know who I am?"

N.Z. (removing pipe): "No."

Officer: "I am an officer!"

N.Z.: "Oh."

Officer: "I—am—an—officer!"

N.Z.: "Well, take an old soldier's advice and don't get drunk and lose your commission."

Officer: "D—— you. Don't you salute an officer when you see one?"

N.Z. (very calmly): "D—— and dot you! It's seldom we salute our own officers, so it isn't likely we'd salute you."

Officer: "Confound it. If you couldn't stand discipline, what did you come out here for?"

N.Z.: "To fight."

Officer (moving on): "I suppose you are one of those damned Colonials."

The R.A.M.C. Sergeant-Major, and other annoyances.

That very great, august and omnipotent being, the Sergeant-Major of this establishment, has just been round. His motto is, I fancy, "*Veni, vidi, vici.*" To him nothing is ever perfect, save himself. He entered, "Shun!" and we stood at attention by our cots. A trembling sergeant and orderly followed in his train. Upon us, one by one, he pounced, this "brave, silent (?) man" at the back. My blue fal-de-lal jacket he unbuttoned and revealed, horror of horrors, very crime of crimes, the fact that I was not wearing the monstrous red scarf which, according to the laws of the R.A.M.C., which alter not, must always be worn by all patients at all times, in life, or even in death, I presume. And further, a most perspiring bare chest revealed the heinous fact that I had omitted to put on the *thick* flannel shirt which has to be worn under the coarse white cotton one. Why wasn't I wearing this article? I explained that I was too hot already. That did not matter a Continental. Where was it? I produced it from under a bed near by and managed to avoid putting it on in his presence, as that would have still further revealed that I was wearing a belt containing money, which is contrary to Rule No. something or other, in which it is emphatically laid down that all jewels, money, and valuables are to be given in to the staff-sergeant in charge of the pack store, who will give a receipt for the same, &c., and so forth. Verily the backbone of the Army is the non-commissioned man, but I must confess to frequently wishing to break, or at least dislocate, that backbone.

The mosquitoes here seem rather more troublesome than their Pretoria relatives. There are twenty men in the next room, and only three of us here; and we three get a frightful lot of attention from these *skeeturs*. They seem vicious as well as hungry. We fancy this is to be explained by the fact that they had been marked down from up country for the base and England, and are enraged at being kept here with the prospect of being returned whence they came; their hunger in this R.A.M.C. Hospital we can understand, and would sympathise with more if they did not treat us as rations. Other patients have a theory that they are the lost and much damned spirits of R.A.M.C. officers, non-commissioned officers, and men, who have gone before and come back to their old earthly billet. But of course these are all mere surmises, and hardly to be regarded seriously. On Thursday I am to be sent to Rondebosch, Tommy's oft and ever-repeated cry, "Roll on, dear old Blighty" (England), seems vainer than ever as time spins out its endless cocoon.

At the Base.

McKenzie's Farm,
Maitland (once again).
Sunday, March 3rd, 1901.

Of late my addresses have been many and varied. The above is the latest. I have filtered through into Maitland, which has changed considerably since last April. On Thursday last I left Wynberg for the convalescent camp at Rondebosch without any regret, for, as a matter of fact, I was getting hungry. On the afternoon of that day I found myself one of a very unselect-looking band of khaki men, parading before the terrible R.A.M.C. Sergt.-Major of the Wynberg Hospital.

Just before parading, I saw the gun carriage, alluded to in my last, being used; going past our ward, in slow time, with reversed arms, went the perspiring and, let us hope not, but I fear 'twas so, the angry Tommies told off as the escort.. Then came the gun carriage with its flag-covered burden. Only another enteric, only another broken heart or so at home, another vacant chair to look at and sigh, and the small but strictly regimental and unsympathetic procession had passed; and the half-interrupted conversation in the ward went gaily on. Having paraded and answered to our names, a doctor strolled down the ranks questioning us, "Are you all right?" All those who answered said "Yes." The question was supposed to be put individually, but by the time he got to where I was, the worthy man was slurring over about three or four at a time. I didn't trouble to reply, it being obviously unnecessary. About half-an-hour later, the ambulance carts came up, which were to bear us to Rondebosch, and we were ordered to carry our kits down and get in. So the halt and the broken picked up their kits—some of them were very heavy—and staggered with them to the carts, a distance of about fifty yards.

In particular, I noticed one poor fellow, a gunner of the 37th Battery, R.F.A. A water cart had gone over him at Mafeking, and fractured three ribs and affected his spine. The poor, emaciated, bent figure of what had once been a smart soldier lifted a rather heavy kit and tottered towards the carts. I felt disgusted at seeing such unnecessary labour thrust on a man, who never should have left the hospital save to go home. But he had been turned out by the powers which be, and—I was going to say shouldn't, but the R.A.M.C. are all honourable men—when I saw a sprightly, well-fed R.A.M.C. Lance-Corporal walking smartly after him, and in a relieved voice I remarked to the man on my left: "The Corporal is going to carry it for him," to which my neighbour remarked: "He can't, he's got a stripe." And, begad, he didn't! He passed him, apparently not having noticed him. I shall have a little more to tell you of the gunner presently.

The drive to Rondebosch, through Wynberg, Kenilworth and Claremont, was lovely beyond words. I had a box seat, and as we drove through the avenues of trees, down the roads, with the gardens of the comfortable-looking bungalows a mass of green foliage and tropical blooms on either side of us, I felt like a gaol-bird escaped from his cage. You may laugh at me if you like, but there I sat with dilating nostrils and eyes, absorbing all I could. Often we passed English girls in white costumes, and pretty, clean-looking children. It was a real treat. Of course, they took no notice of us. We were a common and not altogether pleasing looking lot, many among us being

"Poor fighting men, broke in her wars."

At last the pleasant drive came to its end, and we entered the Rondebosch camp. I was told off with 25 others to a hut, drew bedding and blankets—which included bugs—had some tea at a coffee bar, looked about, and turned in for the night. Alas! that night and others. Rondebosch boasts of a dry canteen and *another*, where Tommy can obtain beer, oftentimes called "Glorious Beer," even as we allude to "Glorious War." Over the sale of this to men, fresh from the hospitals recovering from enteric, wounds, and so forth, there is no restriction. The result needs no imagination—copious libations, songs, rows, and vomitings.

The next day I was put on as Orderly Sergeant. Now, if I was Sergeant-Major and had among my subordinate "non-coms." a man I wished to get into trouble, I should make him an Orderly Sergeant at Rondebosch. About every half-hour the bugles went "Orderly Sergeants," and up I doubled. In all, I attended about a score of these summonses, and even then omitted to report a man who had been absent since *reveillé*.

This last sin of omission came about in this way. I was anxious to turn in early and get a little sleep if possible, but could not do so, as I had to report "all present and correct" at tattoo. Anyhow, I strolled down to our hut at nine o'clock and found that the poor gunner alluded to already was in great pain, writhing about and groaning horribly. One of his chums who was with him told me he could not find a doctor, and the chaplain, who had looked in, had said that he could not get him even a drop of hot water.

The poor fellow was really bad, and thought he was going out, and I should not have been surprised if he had. Soon a few more chums came in, somewhat beery, and commenced to buck him up. The great method apparently on such occasions is to grip the sufferer's hand very tightly, pull him about a good deal, punch him now and again, and tell him to bear up. "Stick it, mate! * * * it, you ain't going to * * * well die! Stick it, mate!" And there he lay, with his pals, fresh from the canteen, exhorting him to stick it, a poor broken Reserve man, with a wife and children across the seas. At last I went and, after no little bother, discovered an R.A.M.C. Sergeant, who found his Sergeant-Major, and the two came with me to our hut. The result was a mustard leaf, which was sent down to me to place on the sufferer. With this on the left side of his stomach, bugs biting, mosquitoes worrying, and comrades lurching in, singing and rowing, and beds collapsing, the night passed. The next day the doctor saw him, and he was returned to Wynberg.*

In the afternoon we paraded and came on here. In the evening I slipped off to Cape Town and met a friend, with whom I dined at the "Grand." Having a decent dinner and amongst decently dressed people made me feel quite a Christian, though as a matter of fact, most of the diners

---

* I met him again looking much better and in the best of spirits on the *Aurania*, being invalided home.

appeared to be Jews. The sheenie man refugee is still very much in evidence, and though he sells things at ruinous prices (for himself, he says) seems to do well.

Tuesday, March 6th. After being kept outside the doctor's bureau from 9 till 12.30, the great man, the controller of fates, the donor of tickets, the Maitland medicine man, has seen me, and, whatever he has done, has not marked me for home.

Another Album ! !

March 9th.

To weary you with a further continuation of the experiences of a forlorn Yeoman, who, having drifted from Pretoria, now finds himself on the sands of Maitland, with a distant and tantalising view of the sea and its ships, seems an unworthy thing to do. But, alas! I have acquired a terrible habit of letter-writing. News or no news, given the opportunity, I religiously once a week contribute to the English mail bag; so here goes for a really short letter.

On Thursday, having endured as much toothache as I deemed expedient without complaint, and goaded on by a sleepless night, I paraded before the doctor, and having borne with him moderately and half satisfied his credulity, obtained from him a note to a Cape Town dentist for the following day. I am now in that being's hands, he has considerately assured me that no man is a hero to his own dentist.

In Cape Town there are two topics—the town guard and the plague, known as bubonic; owing to the latter, great is the stink of disinfectants.

I have already made allusions to the "Sisters' Albums" and the contributions which they levied. Here at McKenzie's Farm, I have struck another style of book. This is run by Sergeant-Major Fownes (10th Hussars) who is in charge of all of the Yeomanry at the base. It is a "Confession Book," containing reasons "Why I joined the Imperial Yeomanry" and "Why I left." It has been contributed to by members of nearly every I.Y. squadron in South Africa. Thanks to the courtesy of its owner, I am able to give you a selection from its contents, omitting the names and squadrons of the contributors only.

WHY I JOINED THE YEOMANRY.

1. To escape my creditors.
2. Patriotism.
3. Because I was sick of England.
4. Could always ride, could always shoot,
   Thought of duty, thought of loot.
5. "England Expects ——" (you know the rest).

6. To injure the Boers.
7. (All Excuses used up.)
8. I considered it was the right thing for an Englishman to do.
9. Because I thought it was my duty.
10. A broken heart.
11. Anxiety to get to South Africa.
12. For the sake of a little excitement, which I can't get at home and didn't get out here.
13. Patriotic Fever!!!
14. I did it during the Patriotic Mania, 1899-1900. Under like circumstances believe I'd do it again.
15. Sudden splash of Patriotism upon visiting a Music Hall.

16. Poetry.
17. "Married in haste."
18. Because I did not bring my aged and respected father up properly.
19. To kill Time and Boers.
20. Because I am Irish and wanted to fight.

21. Love of War.
22. For Sport.
23. My Country's call my ardour fired.

WHY I LEFT.

1. The old man stumped up and I am in no danger of receiving a blue paper.
2. Captured at Lindley. Too much mealie porridge and rice.
3. Because I have changed my mind.
4. Gammy leg, couldn't ride,
   Sent to Cape Town, had to slide.
5. "Go not too often into thy neighbour's house, lest he be weary of thee!"

   HOSPITALS.
   1. Imperial Yeomanry Field. 2. Johannesburg Civil. 3. No. 6 General. 4. No. 9 General. 5. No. 8 General. 6. Deelfontein. 7. Maitland.

6. Because they injured me.
7. Love of my native land (England).
8. I did not get enough fighting, but too much messing about.
9. "FED UP!!!"
10. A broken leg (more serious and imperative).
11. Anxiety to get away from it.
12. Joined B.P.'s Police Force to still search for the impossible.
13. Enteric Fever!!!
14. Ill health.

15. Bathing one day, found varicose veins much to my delight. Invalided.
16. Prose.
17. "Repented at leisure."
18. To see if he has improved.

19. Because Time and Boers wait for no man.
20. Because I want to do more fighting and am joining the S.A.C.
21. Love of Peace.
22. Time for close season.
23. The "Crisis" o'er, I've now retired.

24. Because I was tired of the Old Country.
25. Old England's Honour, Glory, Fame,
    Such thoughts were in my mind.
    To die the last but not disgraced,
    A V.C. perhaps to find.
    To sound the charge, to meet the foe,
    To win or wounded lie,
    My firstborn son and I should fight
    And, if the needs be, die.

26. Hungry for a fight.
27. Drink and Drink.
28. Vanity.
29. Because I thought:
    [1] 'Twas a glorious life on the veldt,
        So unrestrained and free. *(Note. Read opposite page.)*
    [2] 'Twas grand to lie 'neath the star-lit sky
        In a blanket warm and nice.
    [3] 'Twas exciting to gallop over the plains
        To the music of the Mausers,
    [4] Bully beef and biscuits are all very well,
        And so, for a time, is jam,
30. To have a lively time.

31. Wanted to see a little of South Africa.
32. Came out on Chance.
33. To escape the Police at home.
34. Had always preached Patriotism and thought it was the time to put theory into practice.
35. Because I had nothing to do at home
    Bar drinking whiskies and sodas alone,
    And shooting pheasants which is beastly slow,
    So I thought I'd give the Bo-ahs a show.
36. Thought I would get the V.C.
37. A soldier's son and a volunteer
    Heaps of glory, bags of beer.
38. To become acquainted with Colonials before settling.
39. For adventure.

40. Northumbria's reply, "Duty."

24. Because I was sick of the New.
25. Alas, no Glory have I earned,
    No Trumpet's Requiem found,
    Altho' I've laid upon the veldt,
    With scanty comfort round.
    My son has seen more fights than I,
    Tho' he is scarce fifteen,
    Whilst I must sound my trumpet at
    The Yeoman's Base-fontein.
            SERGT.-TRUMPETER (McKenzie's Farm).
26. Appetite appeased.
27. Drink and Drink.
28. Vexation of Spirit.
29. But I found:
    1. That after twelve months of the same I felt
       It was not the life for me.
    2. That when you wanted to go to sleep,
       You're scratching and hunting for l—ce.
    3. That 'twas very unpleasant to ride all day
       When you'd lost the seat of your trousers.
    4. That to get nothing else for more than six months,
       Would make any fellow say "D——!"
30. What with Mausers by day and crawlers by night. I had it.
31. Have seen enough.
32. Going home to a Certainty.
33. Same reason here.
34. The Patriotic Fever has run its natural course.
35. Because the Bo-ahs shot me instead,
    And the papers (confound them) reported me "dead,"
    That sort of game is rather too bad,
    So the prodigal now returns to his dad.
36. Got C.B. instead!
37. Bags of biscuits hard as rocks,
    Smashed my teeth and gave me sox!
38. To join the Bodyguard for same reason and—*better pay*.
39. To go back to a hum-drum life, which is better than a Dum-Dum death.
40. Novelty somewhat worn off, and military discipline not being at all adapted to my temperament.

In a few days all the men marked for home will be leaving, and to those they will be leaving behind them the yearning to be on the sea once again, seems stronger than ever,

"Can you hear the crash on her bows, dear lass,
 And the drum of the racing screw,
 As she ships it green on the old trail, our own trail, the home trail,
 As she lifts and 'scends on the long trail—the trail that is always new?"

Home.

ENGLAND-FONTEIN.

April 22nd, 1901.

"We're goin' 'ome, we're goin' 'ome,
 Our ship is at the shore,
 An' you must pack your 'aversack,
 For we won't come back no more."

So from going up to Elandsfontein, which is by Johannesburg, it came to the above cheerful sentiment. And this is how it happened. An order came from somewhere to our doctor, who had of late so hardened his heart, to "invalid convalescents freely," and, to be brief, within a few days nearly every man at Maitland was marked for home, wore a smiling face, and drew warm clothes for the voyage.

The next burning questions were "What boat will it be and when does she sail?" Needless to say, these interrogatories were answered at least thrice a day, and were always wide of the mark. Still, we were booked for home, and could afford to wait cheerfully. Our hut (No. 1), inhabited by the thirty best men in the camp (any man of that hut will tell you this assertion is correct), thereupon blossomed forth as the publishing and editorial offices of a camp newspaper known as the

"LATEST DEVELOPMENTS GAZETTE,"
WITH WHICH IS INCORPORATED
"THE COOKHOUSE NEWS."

In this journal shipping intelligence was a speciality, and topical cartoons a great feature. We claimed the largest circulation in the camp. The various articles, stop-press news, and cartoons, were stuck on the walls of the hut and afforded much entertainment. Of course, B.P. was very unpopular in Cape Town and with us, and had to be dealt with severely. (Note.—Not the Mafeking man or the "worth a guinea a box" lot, but the Bubonic Plague).

A few days before sailing I caught sight of a well-known name in the dread casualty list: "69th Co. I.Y., 16,424, Trooper R. Blake, (severely wounded, since dead). Hartebeestefontein." "Poor Blake! He used to sing at our concerts on the boat coming out, at our bivouac fire when we indulged in an impromptu sing-song, and at Pretoria, when in the police, he often appeared at the various musical entertainments held in the town or hospitals. His mimicry of a growling or barking dog, big or small, was marvellous and notorious. I remember once how a fellow on one occasion, accustomed to Master Blake's games, on hearing a persistent yapping at his heels, at length said "Oh, shut up, young Blake!" and turned round to see a live terrier there. A verse in the last issue of our paper, expressed, in a humble way, every man's feelings on such matters.

> We are leaving them behind us,
>   'Neath the veldt and by the town,
> The men who joined and fought with us,
>   Who shared each up and down.
> We are going home without them,
>   But our thoughts will on them dwell,
> We shall often talk about them,
>   Good comrades all, farewell!

The day before we left, the sketches and other matter were sold by auction, it having been previously decided to devote the proceeds of the sale to the last No. 1 Hut annual ball. By way of explanation, it must be noted that the hut had an annual ball *once a week*, "dancing strictly prohibited." To be explicit, the annual ball was a weekly dinner. The auction was a great success, a real auctioneer presiding, well over £10 being realised.

The farewell dinner was a grand affair and very convivial. To my surprise I was presented with a handsome silver cigarette case by the so-called staff of the "L. D. News" as a token of good will and their appreciation of my humble efforts to relieve the monotony of camp life.

The next day, Friday, March 29th, we embarked on the transport "Aurania," and, as the sun was setting, bade a sarcastic good-bye to Table Mountain.

As regards the voyage home, which was accomplished in three weeks, much might be said, but probably little of particular interest. A transport is not a very luxurious affair for the common soldier, though the accommodation for the officers amply atones for what may be lacking for the ninety-and-nine, as it were. But what on earth, or sea, did it matter, we were going home.

Good Friday was not a success, an officer committed suicide, a sergeant in the Royal Sussex died of dysentery, the engines broke down, and we had no buns. At St. Vincent we stopped two-and-a-half days to coal, and flew the yellow flag at the fore, being in quarantine on account of the Bubonic outbreak at Cape Town. In the Bay of Biscay a Yeoman comrade died of enteric, and was buried two days from home. Friday, the 18th, on a lovely spring morning, the sea being as smooth as glass, we sighted the cliffs of England once again.

"England, my England."

Then we commenced passing shipping; a man at the tiller of a Cornish fishing boat waving his cap to us made it clear that we were getting back to our real ain folk once more. At eight in the evening we were lying off Netley Hospital, and taking in the proffered advice of a large board in a field by the waterside to eat Quaker Oats, and by twelve o'clock the following night I was home once again.

The treking, the fighting, the guards and pickets, the hospitals are done with now. My small part in the game has been played, and, with a slight and permissible alteration, the concluding lines of a favourite poem must end these simple records.

"But to-day I leave the Army, shall I curse its service then?
God be thanked, whate'er comes after, I have lived and toiled with men!"

THE END.

BURFIELD & PENNELLS, PRINTERS, HASTINGS.